A Child's Book of Warriors

William Canton

Illustrated by Herbert Cole

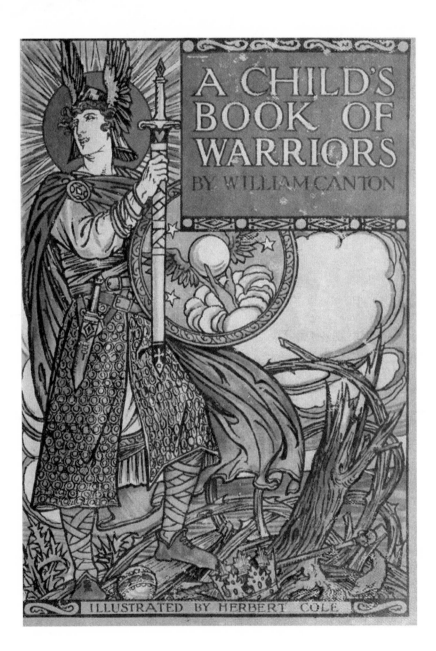

A CHILD'S BOOK OF WARRIORS

BY WILLIAM CANTON

ILLUSTRATED BY HERBERT COLE

A GIRL WAS SINGING HALF HIDDEN AMONG
THE BRIGHT GREEN LEAVES OF THE
TREES AND THE PRINCE CHECKED
HIS HORSE TO LISTEN TO HER

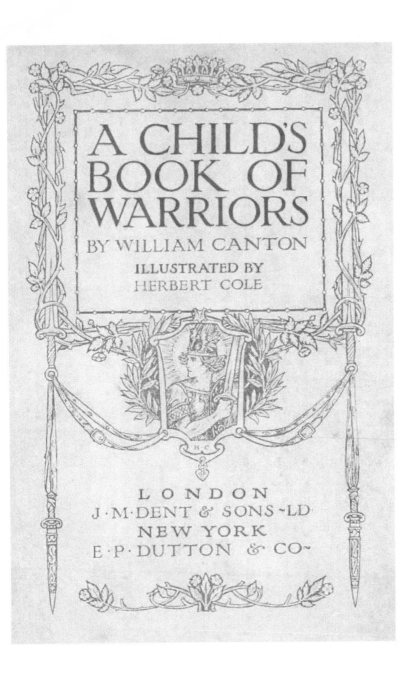

A CHILD'S BOOK OF WARRIORS

BY WILLIAM CANTON

ILLUSTRATED BY
HERBERT COLE

LONDON
J·M·DENT & SONS~LD
NEW YORK
E·P·DUTTON & CO~

TO URSULA

For you who love heroic things
    In summer dream or winter tale,
I tell of warriors, saints, and kings,
    In scarlet, sackcloth, glittering mail,
And helmets peaked with iron wings.

They beat down Wrong; they strove for Right,
    In ringing fields, on grappled ships,
Singing they flung into the fight;
    They fell with triumph on their lips,
And in their eyes a glorious light.

That light still gleams.   From far away
    Their brave song greets us like a cheer.
We fight the same great fight as they,
    Right against Wrong; we, now and here;
They, in their fashion, yesterday.

CONTENTS

THE ROCK OF NARSINGA

THIS was the first of the stories told in the garden at Sebertswold.

Very few people know, said the Truthful Storyteller, how the great King Alexander came to the Rock of Narsinga; how the hill folk, deeming their rock impregnable, made a mock of him; and what befell them and made their lives bitter for many a long year afterwards.

It was in the course of that marvellous invasion in which Alexander, bent upon achieving the lordship of the world, set in his crown the golden horns of East and West, and the peoples he conquered, unable to pronounce his Greek name, and seeing on his head the symbols of his power, called him Iskander Dulkarnein, Iskander the Two-horned.

He had crossed the blinding wastes of salt and sand in the autumn, and had reached the edge of the hill country. During the great cold his legions lay round their camp-fires in the orchards and meadows of the Uzbeks; but at the first sign of spring, when almond-blossom breaks, he marched through the mountains to Narsinga, the Valley of the Sun. Winter was still white on the high pine woods and on the half-circle of peaks which shut in the valley; and the route eastward over the mountains was spear-deep in snow. At the foot of the pass the rock sprang up in precipitous cliffs. There was no foothold except upon one side where a track had been hewn in narrow steps to the stronghold on the summit, and there the wives and children of

1

the hill chiefs had been sent for safety, with a band of valiant tribesmen to defend them.

With a proud clamour of trumpets, the heralds of Iskander called for submission, and promised in return for prompt surrender, peace and unravaged fields, freedom to return to their homes, and alliance with the great king. "But if you will not, then shall he who hath shaken the snow from cities covered by the northern cold, let in the light on nations underground, and crossed the waters on bridges of the slain, wax wroth and harry your eyrie, and make your tribes his bondsmen for ever."

Then from the rock came a barbarous peal of laughter, and the mountains awoke and flung to each other the echoes of that fierce derision; and Oxyart the Bactrian leaped upon the wall of the fort and cried down to the heralds: "Is Dulkarnein lord of the rainbow that he can come to us? Or are his warriors winged that they can capture this mountain for him? None other do we fear." And once again the cliffs of Narsinga rang with mocking laughter.

Who but Dulkarnein reddened with anger? He had a splendid reward cried through the camp—twelve talents of gold for the first man, and thrice a hundred Darics for the tenth, who scaled the Rock of Narsinga. Adventurers were not wanting. Three hundred threw in their lot for the daring feat. They chose the side where the cliffs were steepest and least guarded; and advancing silently in the starlight, they planted ladders of pine, drove iron tent-pegs into the ice and the hard ground, and knotting ropes to the pegs, drew themselves up the face of the rock.

A tithe perished in that wild climbing—broken on the rocks or lost in the chasms of snow; but the rest reached the top as the grey dawn broke. They piled up the small faggots they had brought, and kindled fire; and as the flame leaped up on the peak, there rose from the darkness of the valley pealing of trumpets and shouting of the legions; and that clamour, as of a mighty wind, struck the hill-folk with panic. Women wailed and children ran shrieking; but the shaggy tribesmen stared motionless at the blaze, and at what seemed a host, half seen in its red light.

Then out of the dark valley was heard the voice of the herald calling: "Ho, you of the rock, give ear! 'See you not my winged warriors?' saith the lord of the rainbow. Cast aside quiver and bow, sword and spear, and yield to the mightiest. Your lives he spares you, man and maid, mother and child; but from this sunrise he counts you among his bondfolk."

So the Rock of Narsinga was taken.

When droves of horses had trampled down the snow in the pass, the legions of that famous invasion streamed over the mountains into the East; and in the midst, between vanguard and rearguard, passed the flower of kings, Iskander of the Two Horns.

But a troop of veterans was left behind upon the rock to hold the tribes in subjection. Twice and yet again the people rose in arms, but the veterans came down into the valley and broke and slew them. In times of peace nothing was seen of these men of iron. No one knew how they fared; whether they were relieved; when they were provisioned. The rock was hated and shunned. Between sunset and dawn the most daring spirit in the hills would have fled from it in terror.

One sure sign there was of the sleepless watch of the garrison. Summer and winter, at noon or at midnight, the sound of their trumpets suddenly rang out from the fort on the rock. At one time it might be a low, plaintive cadence which floated across the valley; at another it was a fierce confusion of alarms and charges and recalls from pursuit.

So the years passed away. The old people died and were laid in the stone chambers of sleep hewn in the cliffs. The boys and girls grew up, and a new race of children played in the Valley of the Sun. And long afterwards, upon a summer evening, the villagers sat under their sacred fig-tree near the little red shrine by the lake-side.

WHO BUT DULKARNEIN REDDENED WITH ANGER.

The fragrance of the pine-woods was keen in the sunny air; and soft as the bloom of a plum the purple light lay upon the peaks. Among the villagers was a venerable elder to whom no one spoke, because he was slumbrous with the dreams of the aged; but as they talked together, some words fell upon his ear and aroused him to sudden and eager attention. His eyes gleamed with a wild, dark light as he questioned them.

The Elder. Was there not one who spoke but now of the Lords of the Rock?

Villagers. Yes, here is one who spoke of them.

The Elder. It may be I did not hear aright. What doth he say?

Old man. He wonders whether the Lords of the Rock be not all dead at last.

The Elder. Dead at last? Wherefore should he wonder? Hath he seen—hath he heard—

Old man. Nay, father of hoariness, he hath listened and hath not heard. He hath hearkened for their trumpets and hath heard them not. The trumpets blow no more.

The Elder. That cannot be. Hath no man heard the wicked cry of the trumpets? Who saith this?

Old man. Here is the young man. Let him answer thee.

The Elder. Speak, O son of wonder; what is this thou say'st of the trumpets?

Youth. In the winter storms I heard them. A little while ago in the great gales late in the spring they were silent. Yet who doth not know that they ever blared fiercest in the wind and tempest?

The Elder. Yea, truth-teller, 'twas in the wild weather they thought it most joy to lift up their voices. "Dulkarnein, Dulkarnein! Ye are his bondfolk, ye are his bondfolk!" 'Twas so they kept calling; by night, by day, in sun-time, in snow-time, but loudest always when the weather was wildest.

Villagers. It may be the lords are all dead at last. (*They come from under the sacred tree and look up curiously to the fort on the rock.*)

Youth. In the winter storms the trumpet-calls seemed to sound fainter than they used to be. Surely, I thought, even the Lords of the Rock are growing old.

Villagers. They must all be very ancient men.

The Elder (who has been gazing at the rock with his wildly lighted eyes). All dead at last? They dead? Do not think it. They are not of flesh as we are; they are men of bronze, men of mill-stone. They will never die.

Old man. All things yield to time and death; and these are very old.

The Elder. Very old, very old! They were veterans when I was still young. O ye gods of the steadfast hills, what valour and what might were theirs! We, the strong men of the cliffs, unconquered since time began, we went down like corn before them; they scattered us like leaves in the fall of the year. Dulkarnein, Dulkarnein!

Villagers. Didst thou look on the Two-Horned, thou warrior of old?

The Elder. Even I. A tall companion he was; and out of the crowned head of him jutted the golden horns. Blue-eyed and yellow-haired, like a god! Wholly comely and radiant in the pride of his youth, save that he bore his neck somewhat awry!" Dulkarnein, Dulkarnein! Ye are his bondfolk!" We rose and they vanquished us. Again and yet again we rose, and the Lords of the Rock came upon us as a hail of fire. They clothed us with shame; they shod us with weakness; they bowed our proud heads with ashes. They sheathed the sword; they quelled our hearts with the trumpet-cry of power. The mountain echoes hooted us for slaves, but our sinews were loosened. Our children grew up in bondage; our children's children were born in bondage. Who among you but now thinks that of all losses the loss of life is the worst?

A Child's Book of Warriors

Villagers. Why, yes; lose life, lose all.

The Elder. And once we were the free men of the hills! Dulkarnein, Dulkarnein!

(*A troop of boys run in shouting joyfully, "The trumpets, the trumpets!" "The Lords of the Rock!" The Elder lifts up his hand for quiet. The lads stand silent and shame faced.*)

The Elder. Let but one speak. You with the bird's nest.

Boy. Peace on thy head, father; on thine eyes, peace! We wondered why the trumpets had so long ceased sounding. We stole through the woods. We scaled the rock. At the top all was so still that we ventured upon the wall.

The Elder. Yet this child was born in bondage!

Boy. There was no one. All the place is tumbling down; it is all grown over with bushes.

The Elder. Speak on; what more?

Boy. Up yonder there are eight big stone trumpets fixed on pillars. They are choked with bird's nests and dead leaves. The wind cannot blow through them now; so they have stopped sounding. This is one of the nests.

The Elder. O ye divine lights of night and day! Boy. The Lords made them long ago, we think—before they marched away.

Boy. The Lords made them long ago, *we* think—before they marched away.

The Elder. And we were the free men of the hills! Hold my hand, friends; mine eyes have grown dark. . . . Dulkarnein! Dulkarnein! . . . My breath fails for anguish. To die is not the worst of life's losses.

(The Elder sinks back in their arms. They lay him down gently under the sacred tree, and cover his face.)

"Now, that's where an aeroplane would have come in," said Giggums, the electrical engineer. "If they'd had a Bleriot, they would have jolly soon spotted that fake of old Iskander and his glittering Myrmidons."

"They didn't need aeroplanes," rejoined Simplicia, "if they'd had great hearts. Did they, father? Why, those boys were braver than they were."

"Boy scouts, I expect," said Giggums. "But, my bananas! wasn't it a cute dodge?"

"It was horribly mean, and tricky, and cruel," cried Simplicia; and Vigdis, who evidently took Simplicia's view of the matter, scornfully flung a handful of rose-leaves over the electrician.

All that afternoon, while the apple-trees glittered red and green, and out on the hillside opposite the great beeches burned in gold and russet, with rings of fallen leaves glowing at their feet like reflections on the grass, we sat and talked of old heroic things "and battles long ago." And many a sunny evening after that; right through to the end of a wonderful September. All the apples were gathered; the martins flocked in thousands, and were up and away by starlight one morning ("Even little chaps like those run two houses," quoth the electrician); the pink flowers of the willow-herb turned into tufts of silvery feathers; and still there were tales to tell, for since time began there have ever been heroes, and all life is warfare by land and sea, and Alexander had little need to weep for worlds to conquer, until he had conquered the turbulent spirit under his own crown.

There were tales of the huge earthworks that you can still see on the lonely downs; tales of legions lost in the forest, for the woodland tribes surrounded them as they marched, and the trees came crashing down on all sides of them, and they were trapped and slain among the fallen timber, and their bones were left to whiten in the gloom of the woods; tales of savage hordes who streamed from the steppes by the hundred thousand, with their wives and children in bullock waggons, seeking for new settlements. They carried all before them until they came to the entrenchment of the Cæsars, and there a single red-plumed horse-soldier turned them aside—so awful was the name of Rome!

Do not suppose we forgot our own great Roman Wall. Simplicia thought there was no romance equal to that of the mighty rampart which swept across the moors from the shipping in the Tyne to the sands of the Solway. She hugged herself with delight as she spoke of the tramp of the sentries and the flashing of spears between the watch-towers. Mile after mile, one looked from the tops of the castles, beyond the rolling heather, to the blue Cheviots. And all along the southern side of the Wall lay the stations—great camps grown into little towns, with white pillars of colonnades glinting through the trees. One liked to imagine them on market-days, full of life and gaiety—folk flocking in from villages and farms, traders and chapmen hawking their wares, merry groups of soldiers watching the jugglers and dancing-girls. Nothing could be more wonderful than those soldiers and their babel of tongues. Spaniards and Syrians, men from Athens and Carthage, Goths from the Baltic and Huns from the Danube, negroes from Nubia and Persians from the Euphrates, they seemed to have come from every country under the sun.

The weather broke early in October, and we had very few stories until Christmas, when Sigfrid, our Iceland friend, came and brought three days of driving snow with him. He rigged up snow-shoes for us, and in his honour we made the fire blaze with old wood from the rose-bushes and loppings from the fruit trees. Then to the huge joy of Vigdis, who pretended that we were in Iceland, and that the Northern Lights were dancing over the white wastes, Sigfrid told us the old Viking sagas.

In the long evenings many of the stories got written down in remembrance of a good time, and I hope they still keep some of the freshness of the garden and the pleasantness of the winter fires.

BALT THE ATTACOT

"THE fairest spot on all the long Wall!" exclaimed Balt the Chapman, and his shrewd, kindly face lit up at the sight of Borcovicus, the great Roman station, glittering white and green on the ridge in the morning sunshine. "Yet I would give somewhat to know how I have been brought hither; to understand what force has been laid upon me—plain as hand on shoulder, turning me aside from my way and pressing me onward;" and Balt's brows were knitted in perplexity as he thought of the unaccountable impulses which had changed the course of his wanderings. Then he threw back his head with a laugh: "Why trouble? There be more that walk the world than they who leave footprints in the dust."

It was a wild, picturesque figure that strode, hunting-spear in hand, beside the string of three pack horses. Broad and thick-set, clad in dark green tunic and deer-skin brogues; with heavy axe in belt, and shaggy red hair tumbling down behind on a short cloak of brown leather, such he was long remembered on the moors and by the woodsides between York city and the Solway shores of his own people.

The day was still at morning when the horses clattered through the town on the slope below the station, and as they stopped before the tavern of Paulus, the old centurion himself came hurrying from the courtyard.

"Ho, Balt! The very man! And how fares it with thee, brave Attacot?"

"And with thee, babe of Rome?" replied Balt, grasping his hand; "but why 'the very man'?"

"Faith, thy calling has sharpened thy wits, Balt. Well, 'tis thus," slipping his arm through the chapman's, and dropping his voice. "These three days I have had a message for thine ears alone. Lucius our Etheling has urgent need of thee, and bade me pray thee hasten to him at Cilurnum."

"So! Cilurnum! I knew the call was to Cilurnum. Canst thou guess the reason for this haste?"

"Nay. I only know that the need was great and the message secret."

"Give me food then, good Paulus, and the grass shall not grow under these feet."

Without more words the beasts were stalled, the packs housed, and cup and trencher laid before the traveller; and as the chapman ate and drank, the two spoke in low voices of what was uppermost in Men's minds. And that was the evil which had fallen upon the Christians; for these were the days in which the Cæsar Galerius was the malignant genius of the empire, and the persecution of Diocletian had begun. Already in the south the earth of Britain had been drenched with the blood of martyrs, and though no one had yet been challenged for his faith in the towns along the Wall, the believers looked with anxious hearts for what each to-morrow might bring forth.

"I tell thee, friend," said Balt, "no man is safe. Every petty magistrate counts on his zeal for favour and profit. Our Caesar, Constantius, hates the edict, but though they say he is himself more than half a Christian, he cannot openly oppose it. Men's lives will be cheap with the sycophant and the secret enemy. But why do I talk when time presses? What I can tell thou shalt hear; for before I go I would have thee write for me to the holy presbyter Martinus. Take thy pen."

And this was Balt's letter to the priest.

"Here am I writing to thee in the house of Paulus. Yet not I, Balt the unlearned, but Paulus writes, heeding well the words I say. As to this edict I pray the One God have thee in His keeping.

"I have travelled far, and my news is grievous, though we in the north have yet been nowise molested. Churches have been destroyed; houses filled with believers have been set on fire; men and women have been bound together and cast into the rivers. So many were slain in one place, they call it now 'the field of dead men.' But of that town, I praise the Lord of heaven and earth, and can tell thee such a portent as thou shalt scarce believe.

"For, look you, when Aurelian the prætor came to the forum with his lictors, they found a great crowd staring with white faces at the judgment-seat. And as the crowd parted, the prætor saw that a naked man sat in the very seat of judgment. His body was bloody with scourging. His head was crowned with thorns. For a moment the lictors stood in amazement; then as they thrust forward to seize the man, he arose and stretched out his hands to stay them; and blood from wounds in his hands fell in great drops. His eyes were fixed upon Aurelian, and so gazing he vanished from sight.

"What thinkst thou, venerable one? That day Aurelian judged no one, and at nightfall he was dead."

"Surely the Lord hath care of His saints," exclaimed Paulus; but Balt continued.

"Many have fled to the forests and the mountains. It grieves me that, being so many, they should have fled. Why did they not think, setting shoulder to shoulder, to make a stand for Christus?

"Here Paulus stays his pen to answer me: 'They that take the sword, with the sword shall they perish.' And they that took no sword, say I, have also perished. 'He died for us,' said Paulus. Wherefore, say I, we *live* for Him; is it not so thou teachest, Martinus?

13

"Till now we have been untroubled here, but no one can foresee what is to come. I hear strange rumours. Before this sun is set I am in Cilurnum, where new things are heard soonest. I know not why I should go thither in such haste. Yet these three days I have been pressed onward. Hast thou ever heard voices in thy sleep, calling thy name, and didst thou know they called thee from such or such a place?

"No more at this time. Balt the Attacot, writing to thee here with Paulus, who writes for me."

Having pondered for a time, chin on hand, "Write again, Paulus," said the chapman.

"Now I bethink me, yonder on the hill at Vindolana (Borcum) they worship Mithras; at Corstorpitum (Corbridge) 'tis Ashtoreth; here Sylvanus of the woods and heaths; there the ancient gods, the mother goddesses—I know not what. Worship any of these, saith the edict; worship what you will, so it be not Christus. Worship Christus, and you die. What bondage and oppression of the soul is this! O Galerius, who hath made thee Cæsar over the thoughts and hearts of men?

"Worship Christus, and you die. Then not without iron in hand. Surely life is a gladsome thing—to drink in the bright air, to see the faces of one's kind, and the flower on the heather, and the light on the blue hills afar. I burn no incense; and I give my life to no man, Cæsar or Augustus. I die not till I must, and then not alone. It makes me mad to think that, being so many, they struck no blow for Christus and the joy of free men. What sayst thou, man of God?"

Eastward from Borcovicus the Great Wall swings from crag to crag along the ridge, which sinks down at last into the green woods of the Tyne valley; but Balt followed the broad way of the legions, which runs direct across the lower ground. Swallows frolicked in the heavens; rabbits scuttled through the broom and bracken; bees droned among the rose-purple tops of the willow-herb; butterflies fluttered round the white flowers of the enchanter's night-shade;

people went by with friendly "good days;" far away on the towered rampart sentries moved to and fro—it was all just the same as he had seen it hundreds of times before. And yet, in some strange fashion, he was aware that everything was changed; and as he fared onward, going he knew not why, and whither he had no will to go, he looked and listened with the interest of a traveller who sees and hears new things that he will not hear or see again.

Near the foot of the hill, where the road runs once more beside the Wall, a man sat on a boulder, drowsing in the hot sun. At the sight of him, Balt flourished his spear with a shout: "Hail, Trebonius Victor." Springing to his feet, the man waved his hand, and ran to meet him. He was a colossal negro, one of the Nubian auxiliaries who had served upon the Wall, and was now in the household of the Etheling. The genial black face, the huge black neck with its torque of gold, the brawny black arms with their silver arm-rings seemed doubly dark against his white woollen tunic.

"Praise to the Giver, thou art come!" he cried. "The master hath long waited for thee. This track through the wood, good Balt, is quickest."

They left the road, and striking through a green brake, plunged into a twilight of oak and beech. The track ended in a sunny clearing, in the midst of which a stockaded earth-ring and deep trench encircled the home of Lucius and of the ancient British princes of his race. Their coming was signalled by a fierce clamour of hounds, until the voice of the Nubian rang out for silence.

At the entrance of the great dyke Lucius met them: "Oh, friend Balt, I am fain to see thee. Much have I prayed to have thee, and the King of heaven hath surely sent thee."

"Wherein can I serve thee, highness?"

"That thou shalt know quickly; but first thou shalt honour this house."

"I will break bread, and I will drink with a proud heart to thee and thy house, but already have I eaten what befits a man."

"This then," said the Etheling, as they sat in the old hall, "is the bitter need in which I ask thy help." And glancing at the wicked terms of the edict, he told how he had been warned that a friend of his youth, now grown to a deadly enemy, had planned to impeach his faith in the gods and his loyalty to the emperor. At any moment, to-day, to-morrow, he might be called forth to burn incense to the idols.

"And thou wouldst draw sword first?" cried Balt with flashing eyes. "O prince, I am thy man. At thy side I stand."

"Nay, Balt, what wild man's thoughts are these? To fight were folly; to flee were shame, and an evil end. I could stand in the face of men and the face of the Maker of men, and bear witness to Him crucified. And at my side Valeria, my wife, unshrinking. But oh, Balt!—my little lad; thou knowest him; he is but six years old joyous as a little bird, fairer than any flower; how could I bear to see him in torture, to see him in the flames, to see him hewn or strangled? Could I but send him to my kinsman, Fortunatus, in the palace at York, there he would be safe, and it would be well with us."

"Didst thou desire me for this? Then, by the Holy One in the heavens," said Balt, raising his hand on high, "I take the child for thee to York, or I perish by the way."

"Wilt thou take him? Oh, Balt, God give thee too a little son to be the joy of thy age. Thou hast lifted our heart out of anguish. Henceforth we shall know but a common sorrow. When canst thou go?"

For a moment the Attacot considered: "The river is not safe. We shall go by the ways of wood and wold. I know each ford, cave, hill-track, moorland gully 'twixt this and Knavesmire. Let it be when midnight has turned. The moon is at full and the dawn is early."

"The Nubian shall go with thee."

"Good! and better if thou wilt let him have a horse and one of thy wolf-hounds."

"O Balt, the poor house is thine; spare for nothing thou canst need."

Bright shone the moon of the summer night on the grassy earthworks and the ancient roof-tree of a princely race. Again and again the little Marcus had been hugged and kissed with fond tears. There was no more to say but "God speed you" when Lucius gripped the men's hands hard, and "God bless you, O true hearts" as the mother caught the child once more to her bosom.

They passed through the dusk and glimmer of the sighing wood, Victor leading the horse, and the little man tripping between Balt and the wolf-hound, with a soft fist crumpled in Balt's fingers. Now they were in the midst of the vast open wonder of a world of misty silver and stillness, and the lad rode on the Nubian's shoulders, and short, black shadows went along the ground with them. Now the moon was sinking; a cold breath came from the east where the grey light was breaking, and Marcus lay asleep on the Nubian's arm in a fold of the cloak drawn close about them. Now the warm morning blazed in the pines, and he awoke to see fire burning among the rocks beside a brook, and breakfast ready.

Such a frolic never had been before as this day in the free air and sun, going onward and still onward, with new things to see every moment. And how good it was to lie on heather under a tree at noon, and then to spring up again, to run, to ride, to walk, to chatter merrily in these summer wilds! They passed by upland villages and saw folk at work in the fields; they splashed through shallow rivers; here and there they spoke to a herdsman with his drove of swine in the glades, or a shepherd-boy on the high pastures. On every summit the men paused to scan the country they had left behind them; and then as they went on again Balt would speak of the land ahead— what streams were to cross; what villages and towns were near, where friends of his were to be found at need; what tracks led down to the great roads.

That night they slept in one of the hill-caves, with Grim's head laid on his paws before a fire at the entrance, and one or other of the men keeping watch by turns. When Marcus folded his little hands, the first tears came with remembrance of home, but the Nubian took him in his arms and comforted him, and the twilight sorrow of childhood ran into the quiet underworld of sleep.

It was the forenoon of the third day, and they had reached the moorland heights beyond the Tees river, when the Nubian, looking back, uttered a cry of warning: "See, see, Balt!" He pointed downward to three mounted figures, a long way distant on the plain beyond the stream. "Spanish horse from Cilurnum, if I know my own hand."

"There is yet time," said Balt, "but let us push on;" and as they hastened through the waste, he gave the Nubian fresh instructions. "Less than an hour beyond where you leave me, for I must stop till the danger is over, a track drops down to Swale Water, and you come to Cataractoni (Catterick). Then to York—God willing—'tis a plain course. Do not linger, and doubt not I shall be with you long ere you win so far."

A mile or more over the heather, their journey would have ended at a long chasm which rent the moorland, but for a frail bridge of pine-trees. Far down in that rocky cleft a foaming torrent leaped and raged over ledge and boulder.

"This timber once cut away," said Balt when they had passed over, "we are safe. Leave Grim with me. Farewell, little hero, till I overtake you. Speed, friend Victor!"

Balt drew his axe from his belt and severed two of the pines on the northern side of the gulf. Returning to the opposite edge he hewed mightily. First one and then a second of the tall trunks bent, snapped, and plunged into the torrent. Then he toiled at the two remaining trees. As they parted and swung down with a crash, the wolf-hound growled and sprang to his feet, and the beat of horses' hoofs came drumming over the turf. A glance served to show that Balt's work had been done well, and the riders drew rein.

"Surrender, in the name of Cæsar!"

"If I would I could not," replied Balt, pointing to the chasm.

"Let me help thee," laughed one of the troopers. He rode a little way back from the brink, wheeled swiftly round, and put his horse into a headlong race. In an instant the hound rushed forward and hurled himself against the wild charge. His fangs closed on the horse's throat in mid-leap, and hound, horse, and man were hurled down the sheer wall of the gulf.

"Good Grim!" cried Balt, "thou too wast Christian and Attacot."

Even as he spoke, another of the troopers rose in the saddle, and a spear flew from his hand. It struck the chapman in the chest. Balt staggered; steadied himself with a desperate effort; sent his axe whirling against his slayer, and reeled through the bracken. He fell against a boulder, and the spear snapped.

Then a mist settled upon the moor—blinding, chilling. Was this death? He struggled with the darkness, with the cold. He grasped the boulder, and tried to gain his feet.

At last, oh joy! he felt a mortal burden fall away from him. The mighty spirit of the Attacot stood panting with life. He had never indeed been truly alive until now! The rapture of life overpowered every other feeling. He was unconscious of place or of time. Whether he had stood there one moment or a hundred years he could not tell. Then he became aware that there was One who stood beside him.

Two-and-twenty years had passed away. It was summer in the Bithynian hills. The chestnut woods were in the flush of June. Sails of many colours flitted upon the breezy waters. High over all, the snowy summits of Olympus floated like a dream. In Nicæa, at the head of the lake, the white storks looked down from the marble tops of the basilica upon such stir and excitement as had never yet been seen in its colonnaded streets. It was the year of that holy synod in which East and West met for the first time to restore the peace of Christendom.

THEN HE BECAME AWARE THAT THERE WAS ONE WHO
STOOD BESIDE HIM.

The voice of Constantine had echoed through the world: "Give me back my tranquil days and my nights free from care, O you ministers of the Most High God, who are destroying the one fold with your needless wrangling over mysteries beyond the subtlety of man." But still the wild songs of Arius drove the people to madness; artisans, tradesmen, sailors took up the ribald tunes in the streets, and the emperor's statues were broken in the fierce encounter of rival mobs. "It was the clash of the rock-giants," said the Bishop of Cæsarea, "the Symplegades, when winter howls down the Hellespont."

There was no choice but to call together the great teachers and examplars of the Church, and bid them settle their bitter dissensions. They came from the ends of the empire—bishops from Spain and the rivers of Assyria, from the Gothic forests and the shores of Mauretania; gaunt desert-fathers who bore the names of the old gods of Egypt; aged confessors whose testimony was written in the seared faces, the scored sides, and the maimed limbs. Such a concourse of the mighty in Israel no man living could hope to see twice in the world.

The streets were thronged with fiery partisans, strangely clad anchorets, disputing philosophers, slaves, travellers, gay citizens, wondering country folk. Excitement and confusion were held in check by the imperial guards.

Beside the portals of the basilica, at the meeting of the four streets from the city gates, the Tribune Marcus, a tall young man of singularly gallant bearing, scanned the passing of the Fathers of the Council. Many were unknown; the names of others were tossed about by the crowd, and curious scraps of gossip reached his ears from the garrulous spectators pressing about him.

"Nicolas! Nicolas!" And the Bishop of Myra, "one of the pillars of the world," goes by with silvery locks and a smile on his broad, ruddy face. Here is a man from the ends of the earth—John, Patriarch of India! This is Spyridion of Cyprus. "They took him from the sheep-cotes to make him bishop, but you may still see him with his crook on the hills." "Theophilus the Goth; those big, blue-eyed barbarians are all for Arius!"

Silence suddenly falls upon the spectators as an old man, frail and tremulous, comes leaning upon the shoulder of a youth, whose radiant face and wonderful auburn hair—the hair of the old-world queens of Egypt—have a touch of angelic brightness.

"Who, friend, are these?" asks Marcus of a bystander.

"The venerable man is Alexander, the Pope of Alexandria. How he has aged; and there is the look of death in his face!"

"And the youth?"

"The youth, as you name him, Sir Tribune, is his Archdeacon Athanasius."

And the dying patriarch moves on with the slight, shining figure, whose genius is to dominate this first universal Synod of the Christian Church, and whose name will be held in remembrance for centuries throughout Christendom.

An uncouth form now goes by, clad in rough goat-skins, and were it not for his clear, humorous eyes, more like a wild being of the woods and hills than a bishop.

"'Tis Jacobus of Edessa, from the Land between the Rivers," another bystander tells Marcus. "Dost thou know, Sir Tribune, that thou may'st see there the face of the Lord, even as He was when He dwelt amongst us? This man, I doubt not, hath often looked upon it."

Before Marcus can reply, an outburst of exclamations and fierce counter-cries greets the appearance of an extremely tall, crazed-looking ascetic in a long sleeveless coat and sandals. With twitching hands, and dim eyes peering through the tangles of grizzled hair that hang about his head and bloodless face, he passes on, muttering to himself. Can this be Arius the Heresiarch, the leader of men, the fanatic who sings and dances the mob of Alexandria into frenzy?

As Marcus gazes after him in amazement, loud shouts hail Paphnutius, the hoary confessor and bishop from the Thebaid. He drags one leg painfully along with the aid of a staff, for long ago the persecutors severed the tendons to prevent his escape from the mines. His right eye had been gouged out with a sword and the socket seared with hot iron; but the left is brilliantly dark, and see how those dusky features are illumined with infinite sweetness and peace!

Marcus thrills with emotion. "This man suffered. My mother, my father died!" All the delight, all the pain, all the broken recollections of his strange boyhood live again in those words.

With the arrival of the emperor Nicæa reached the height of splendour and enthusiasm. The synod was transferred to the palace. In the midst of the great hall the Holy Gospels were laid upon a throne of gold, as a visible image of the presence of Christ Himself. Constantine entered, without guards or attendants, and the venerable assembly rose to pay their homage.

What man had ever more truly looked the Master of the World? Great-statured, nobly featured, he surveyed the gathering with bright leonine glances. His long yellow hair, bound with a fillet of pearls, waved on his broad shoulders. A robe of purple silk, ablaze with barbaric gems and flowers of gold, fell to his scarlet shoes.

He stood, blushing, until by their bowing they had motioned him to be seated, and then, in a singularly sweet voice, he besought them to do away with all causes of disagreement and to dissolve every knot of controversy. Unbuckling his sword, he gave it with his ring and sceptre into their keeping; he was but a fellow servant of their common Lord and Saviour. A brazier was brought into the hall, and burning before them unread all the complaints, accusations, and petitions he had received, "Is it not the word of Christ," he asked, "that he who would be forgiven should first forgive his brother?"

The discussion of the great controversy had hardly been begun when wild rumours flew through Nicæa that Arius had stood forth and denied the divinity of Christ—had declared that there was a time when the Son of God did not exist; that God had created Him; and that, being a creature, He might have fallen and sinned through the frailty of His created nature. Many of the bishops had stopped their ears in horror, but Nicolas of Myra had leaped from his seat and struck the blasphemer in the mouth. Nicolas had been deposed for his violence and was now in bonds.

At length there came a day when Arius had fled, and his book of songs denying the eternal Sonship of the Lord was cast into the flames; and the bishops, girding Constantine with the sword he had put into their keeping, laid in his hands the parchment on which Athanasius had copied the Creed of Nicæa:

"We believe in one God, the Father Almighty, Maker of all things visible and invisible . . ."

This was the turning-point in the life of Marcus.

In Rome he had seen the godless splendour, the vicious luxury, the laughing paganism of an age which was crumbling into the abyss. In Nicæa he beheld the pageantry of a Christianity so torn asunder with passionate wranglings and bitter hatreds that there seemed to be no place in it for Christ Himself, the divine Shepherd who led His flock to still waters and carried the lambs in His bosom.

He resigned his sword, and for seventeen years he dwelt with the monks of Nematea in one of the ruined temples near the Nile. Over his head, bowed down in prayer, avenues of sphynxes gazed with stony eyes into the silence of the desert. Brightly coloured processions of Egyptian men and women sang to him a soundless dirge of dead men, of dead women, of dead delights, of the dust and ashes of a vanished race. Like his brethren he wove palm-leaf baskets, crossed the great river to sell them, to hire himself out as a labourer at harvest-time, to share the sorrows of the poor villagers, to worship with them at the same rude altars.

Thereafter he went forth into the mountains of the eastern wilderness where Paul the Hermit had lived and died. The place was an oasis, open to the sky, set among the rocks of an ancient crater. A clear fountain gushed from a cleft in the rocks, and palm trees grew there. He was given charge of the monastery garden, and cultivated herbs and fruits, thinking with a quiet joy that the Lord Himself was once taken for a gardener.

There the days of his years were spent in labour and prayer, and his spirit was upheld by the sweet ministry of created things. For if he looked over the hill-tops into the bright immeasurable distances until sight itself was lost in the intense shining of the desert, why so would it be when the soul stood at gaze before the divine splendour. When the sun went westering and the light abated, far hills rose up in the desert, wonderful as a mirage yet sure and steadfast; why, even thus, when our day declines, shall we discern fair forms of truth which were invisible in the glare and heat. Then in the rosy sundown an owl flitted from tamarind to tamarind; like wisdom making profit of the bitter trees of life.

Thereafter as the sun dropped lower and lower, and the rim of the desert smouldered red, shadows passed over with the murmur of innumerable wings—first one and then a second flight, followed by a third and yet a fourth flight of goldfinches, which came every evening from the palms of the north to those of the south. In the passage of these Marcus took such pure joy that there was no room for other thought or feeling. The wilderness gloomed, but the high heavens were still luminous; and winding and doubling, crossing and making wheels within wheels, the pelicans and flamingos sailed overhead until they faded into trails of shadow; and far into the night Marcus sat in the darkness of his cell, weaving rushes and reciting psalms.

Now it chanced that Marcus had planted a fig-tree, and it had waxed great and fruitful. In his old age, when his years fell little short of ninety, Macarius, the abbot of that desert, came to the oasis; and Marcus led him to the great tree, saying: "This was of my planting and watering; and the fruit is of exceeding virtue — yet I know not, for never yet have I tasted it." "Yea?" said Macarius, musing for a little while; "take thine axe and cut it down."

The old gardener's hands were lifted up in dismay; but he spoke no word and fetched the axe. "Give it to me," said the abbot, taking compassion on the troubled heart of age; "we will not harm the tree, seeing that it is a gift of God." But Marcus answered: "Woe is me, for I have sinned, "and fell at the abbot's feet. "O brother," said Macarius, "it was not so hard to fight with Constantine against barbarians as it is to fight against one's own will. Yet 'tis in the same sign that we shall conquer." And the sign he spoke of was the cross which appeared in the heavens to Constantine.

When evening came, Marcus went up into the heights and beheld the hills ascend out of the desert. But lo! while he looked, their colour changed from dreamy blue and rose to green and russet, and they rolled up over against him in a vast naked moorland. And this change was a miracle.

Full eighty years had gone by, yet it seemed but as yesterday that he was a little lad on that wild heath. There yawned the chasm cloven deep through the moorland rock. Near the brink a man stood beside a boulder. Marcus recognised him; a long-forgotten name sprang to his lips, and he uttered a great cry.

The cry was heard below in the oasis, and the brethren ran from their cells in the rocks, fearing that some ill had befallen him.

"O Balt, is it you? Are you too still alive?"

The Attacot made no answer. But the soul of Marcus was illumined, and in that instant the mystery of the world was made clear to him. And he understood how Balt, in his clinging delight in existence—Balt, who would fight to the death for Christ, but would not freely die for any one, had stood for all these years upon the spot where he was slain; alive, yet not living; kept apart, in a trance of being, from the illimitable life that follows death.

Then out upon the moorland Marcus was aware that there was One who stood beside the Attacot, speaking to him; and Marcus heard the words.

"So slow has thou been to come to me that now I am constrained to come to thee."

Balt seemed to waken suddenly from a trance; his face shone, and he spread abroad his arms, crying, "Lord, my Christus!"

And Christ said: "Dost thou still so cling to thyself that thou wilt not die until thou must?"

"Lord," Balt answered, "I was but a savage man. Now I see Thee; now I know Thee. My will is Thy will to live or to die."

"O Balt," said the Lord, "I am Life. Thou shalt not die; yet, as men count death, already thou hast long been dead. Look down at thy feet."

Marcus looked down at Balt's feet, and he saw, even as Balt saw, the bones of a man which lay white in the bracken; and wedged in the crate of the chest was the head of a spear.

The brethren found Marcus fallen on the hill, and when they thought to lift him, he besought them, "Forbear, dear brethren. This is my Pisgah. Suffer me to die where I have seen the Lord;" and he told them of his vision. Then, as the breath fluttered upon his lips, "Watch with me," he said, "and pray, that I fail not at the last."

The sun dropped. The desert darkened. Overhead in the shining of the high air the pelicans and flamingos made wheels of white within wheels of rose; but before they faded into shadowy trails the old man's eyes glazed, and Marcus was once more with Balt, and both were with Christ.

HOW THEY SAVED NISIBIS

THIS is the story of Jacobus of Edessa, who came in his rough goat-skin and took his place amid the splendour of the Synod of Nicæa, more like a wild creature of the woods than a bishop.

Loath had he been to forego his hermit life among the Masian Mountains, where he had lived on wild herbs, nuts, and berries; his drink had been the torrent; his bed in summer the earth, with the leaves of the forest as a covert against the planets that strike and the blindness that comes of the light of the moon; but in winter, when the great cold which is the sister of death was abroad on the heights, he took shelter in a cave hewn out of the rock.

Amid the peace and gladness of that lonely life, his nearness to God brought him nearer to men, and most of all he loved the people of Nisibis, the city of his birth. Far below upon the plain, in the Land between the Rivers, it lay glittering within the strength of its triple brown walls; wide orchards and gardens and fruitful fields around it; and Mygdon, the blue river, flowing through the midst. Fair as it seemed in the beauty of youth, this was one of the ancient cities on the earth—as old as Nimrod; and Jacobus would stand on a cliff, gazing fondly down upon it, but he refused to be its bishop.

At last his reluctance was overcome by the words of an old gardener, who said to him: "Have I leave to speak? Lo, then, I have a lad, and

29

when I bid him to keep the foxes from the vines, he answereth me, 'Master, I go a-fishing for thee in the pools of Mygdon;' and when I would have him among the orange-trees, 'Master,' he saith, 'there is need that I gather thee fuel for the pot.'" And as Jacobus smiled, "O servant of God," said the gardener, "what will it avail thee to pray in the mountain, if God would have thee for His work in the busy streets?" So Jacobus was made bishop; but he would not lay aside his hermit garb, "Lest," he said, "I should forget the hole of the pit whence I was digged;" and he continued to live as of old on meagre fare and scant sleep, and was ever ministering among his people.

When long years had passed since the great synod, the Emperor Constantine died. He was carried to the Byzantium he had built on the edges of two continents, and in his tomb they laid him in the porch of the Church of the Apostles. Thus did the Master of the World watch as a doorkeeper in the house of the holy fishermen.

While he lived the very shadow of his sword held the world in awe; now that the strong hand had turned to clay sedition spread among the troops of the empire, the worshippers of the sun rose in fury against the Christians, and Sapor, Sultan of Persia, took the field to recover his lost provinces.

The Land between the Rivers seemed an easy conquest and a rich spoil. Nisibis on the frontier barred the way. Twice he besieged it, and twice he was driven back. For the third attack his summons roused the depths of the East. A mighty array swept across the floating bridges of the Tigris—hordes of Tartar horsemen who used the lasso and scalping knife; hill-tribes of the Five Rivers who were armed with bamboo bows and crane-skin shields; Indian kings with troops of elephants bearing towers on their backs; long trains of engines of war. Scarcely visible in the clouds of white dust, legion followed legion to the clash of barbaric music.

The immense host closed with a multitude of women, slaves, servants, whole families with their children and their aged folk. It was a migration rather than a campaign, for these families were to be the first settlers in Nisibis when its champions had been impaled round the walls and its citizens driven with whips into exile. For miles around the clamour and tramp of that invasion sounded like the hoarse roar of the sea, heard far inland on a frosty night.

THEN JACOBUS ASCENDED THE WATCH-TOWER AND LIFTING HIS ARMS TO HEAVEN CHANTED IN A LOUD VOICE, "LET GOD ARISE AND LET HIS ENEMIES BE SCATTERED."

Lucilian was the Governor of Nisibis, but its real defender was the Bishop Jacobus. At the first news of the advance he assembled the inhabitants, distributed arrows, and manned the walls; and his voice rang through the city with the proud cheer of a valiant heart: "O you men of Nisibis, are not these the worshippers of the sun, whom you have driven once and yet again from your walls? They come a third time, and yet a third time will you blacken their faces. They will encompass you, and sit about the city like vultures about a camel fallen on the sand of the desert, but why should you fear? Stand fast, strike, laughing for joy, for the Lord God will give them into your hands, even He who made the sun. Quit you as mighty men, knowing that twice you cannot die and once you cannot miss. Who saith they are many and strong? Nay, if need be, your eyes shall be opened and you shall see the mountain, even Masius yonder, full of horses and chariots of fire."

Day and night Jacobus prayed, and Ephrem, the Syrian Deacon, went among the people, heartening them greatly. And the hosts of Sapor closed about Nisibis, and filled the gardens and orchards and the fields of rice and wheat. But when many days had passed, and the great war-engines were beaten back from the walls, and the elephants strove in vain to break down the gates with brazen rams, and fire and iron came like hail from the towers, Sapor turned the course of the river, thinking to reduce the city by thirst.

When that failed, for there were many wells, he cast earthen dikes about Mygdon, huge and high, and gathered his waters to a mighty head; and when the ripples began to run over the mounds, he loosened the waters. They burst in a booming flood upon Nisibis; the wall of sun-dried bricks rocked, and for the space of a hundred cubits it fell in a mass, but before the Persian hordes could mount to the assault there broke upon them wind and rain such as no man could withstand, and through the storm raced thunder and lightning, as it were horses and chariots of fire.

All that night the men of Nisibis stood with Jacobus and Ephrem in the wide breach, and behind them the citizens reared a new wall to the height of five cubits. At sunrise drums and cymbals sounded the onset, when suddenly upon the rampart appeared a stately form in the dazzle of the morning. It was Jacobus, golden-mitred and robed in episcopal purple. The barbaric music ceased, and dismay checked the assailants. For a moment the priests of the sun thought it had been the imperial spirit of Constantine himself come to the rescue of the city.

Once again the cymbals clashed amid the beating drums, and the heavy cavalry led the wild swarms to the breach; but the rushing waters had left unseen chasms which swallowed horse and man, and tracts of mud in which they floundered and sank. The dead became a bridge for the living, and still the hordes struggled on.

Then Jacobus ascended the watch-tower, and lifting his arms to heaven chanted in a loud voice—

"Let God arise, let His enemies be scattered;"

and below, on the new wall, that cry was taken up by the warriors of Nisibis. Yet louder than the song and the tumult of the onset was heard a sound of hissing, as when the bee-keeper beside the hives hisses for his bees. And the zimb-fly heard it, and came out of the south. As he came, the earth was filled with his humming. He came as a little cloud, which spread and darkened the sun. In myriads he fell on the Persian, man and beast. Horses threw their riders and trampled down the dense ranks about them. Screaming with pain, the castled elephants cut their way with the scythes fastened to their trunks, turned upon each other, and died raging. An agonising rabble, unable to advance or to retreat, the forlorn hope of Sapor shrieked and perished under the dark cloud of the zimb-fly.

The sultan leaped from his high throne. "Death to thee, God of the Romans!" he cried, and bending his bow, shot an arrow into the heavens. Then he mounted the great Horse of the Sun and fled, leaving twenty thousand slain under the towers of Nisibis.

In that year Jacobus slept in Christ, and the city, weeping, buried him in his raiment of goat-skin; but Ephrem the Deacon lived to an old age white as the almond-blossom, and left many hymns and songs and glowing discourses, which may still be read in printed tomes of Latin, Greek, and Syriac. And though himself lowly of spirit, it was he who made the fair young daughter of the Governor of Edessa promise that never again should she enter a litter carried by slaves, for, said he, "The neck of man should bear no yoke save that of Christ."

HERVÉ AND CHRISTINA

IT was in the days of the Saxon conquest, and as the invaders pushed onward into the west, St. Gildas left the holy island of Avalon, and coming to Armorica he founded a monastery on the peninsula which shuts in the rock-sown waters of the Morbihan. Within his view lay the wooded isle in which his beloved Kadoc had made himself a home and had built a granite causeway to the shore, for the children who thronged to his school from the main land. It was among the oaks and pines of Rhuys that his companion Taliesin sang his mystic songs; in the sunny cloister by the blue sea he himself wrote the story of the Overthrow.

"That conquest," he would say, "was a fire which raged across Britain till it slaked its red tongue in the waters of the sunset." Swords gleamed and flames crackled. Fields and farms were wasted. Pitiful it was to see the slain lying in the streets among tumbled columns and broken altars and the tops of high towers. Many hid themselves in the hills and the dark forests, until hunger drove them back, to become the serfs of the conquerors. Multitudes fled to the sea-shore. They crowded into the frail boats covered with bull's hide; their priests led them forth into the deep; they sat under the swelling of the sails and howled in misery: "Thou hast given us, O God, like sheep for meat, and hast scattered us among the heathen."

Among the fugitives in that sorrowful exodus was the young bard Huvarnion. Tall and winsome, master of many tongues, and skilled in all the craft of music and verse, he found a welcome among the famous gleemen who frequented the court of Childebert, King of the Franks. Paris he saw when it was still Lutetia, the strong little island-city of the Seine; and he passed in the king's retinue to more than one of the immense farms which the Franks liked better than any walled town. There they fleeted the time gaily in hunting and fishing and swimming. For the great feast at night the boar and fallow-deer were roasted whole, and in the oak-pillared hall saga and song and the sound of harp and rote alone checked the merriment over the beer-horns and silver wine-cups.

But the heart of Huvarnion was often far away among the hills beyond Severn, and when at length tidings came of a mighty battle in which the heathen had been broken and scattered, the bread of exile became too bitter and he could remain no longer. "You have leave to go," said Childebert, "for every man loves best the dust he played in as a child;" and the king gladdened him with costly gifts, and gave him a letter to the High Chief of Armorica, to speed him overseas.

So Huvarnion reached the coast of Leon, and would indeed have sailed, but that thrice he saw in dreams a maiden more sweet and fair than awake he had ever seen. She stood singing in the glitter of the morning beside a spring on the heath, and her song was of her quest for simples—Joy-wort for the heavy-hearted, and Herb Eye-bright for the blind, and the red Cross-flower which prevents death. After his third dream Huvarnion rose from sleep. The sunny mist was drifting from the heath. Far away he heard her singing, and beside a clear spring he found her. Her name was Rivanon, and like himself she was a minstrel. After a brief wooing there was a joyful wedding.

When their little son was born and they saw that he was blind, they wept over him in his mother's arms, and called him Hervé, which is "bitterness." But love sweetened the bitterness. The child throve and grew strong and bright in a home where music was never silent. He was still very young when he began to touch the harp-strings, and his father made him such an instrument as he could play. Then, as he grew bigger and little tunes came to him, "O mother," he would cry, "isn't this like wild roses on the brambles?" or "Listen, mother; would you say that was moonlight?"

He was scarcely six years old when Huvarnion died; and in the autumn after that year Rivanon fell ill and lost her strength. One day Hervé took her hands and placed them upon his shoulders: "See how big and brave I am. Now you must let me go out and beg for you." She drew him to her and cried quietly, but the lad had his way. His little white dog led him to the villages and farms, where he sang the many songs his mother had taught him. The folk were good to him, but there were cruel days in the white winter when he could hardly sing at all for the chattering of his teeth with cold, and his bare feet left red tracks in the snow; and when he reached home again, he just fell back into the little child, and Rivanon nursed him on her lap and sang and cried him to sleep.

When he was about fourteen or fifteen he spoke to her of the great longing that was in his heart. "Sometimes I think I am like one of those birds which are blinded that they may sing the more constantly. And oh, mother, how happy would it be for me if a hermitage were to be my cage; and would it not make God look glad to hear me singing for Him at all times?"

"That perhaps may be God's will, dear son," said Rivanon; and she sent him to his great-uncle Gourfoed, who was a solitary in the forest of the Red Stones. The old man blessed him, and received him with joy among his disciples; but Rivanon joined a sisterhood of holy women who tended the sick and solaced the aged and sorrowful.

Oh, the blithe school-days in the forest, when one could scarce believe that Hervé was blind! For he seemed to be the very spirit of light, his face shone, and he fared as though he saw things by the brightness of his soul. He came to know the letters by shape and touch, so that he might teach others. His memory was like a wonderful book, in which the Scriptures were written day by day;

and all manner of skill and deftness lived in his fingers. Out-of-doors he could tell the names of the trees by their sound in the wind; he was guided by their scent to the places where herbs and wild flowers grew; and never a bird or beast was there but came to him at call. When a wolf killed his little white dog, he put its leash on the savage creature, and bade him listen: "It is your turn now, Wolf, to lead the blind. People have a saying, 'Like the wolf, which is grey before he is good,' but you must be good now and ever after." And the wolf looked up into his sightless eyes, and in them he saw something that tamed him.

One day of days, when Hervé was grown up, his mother came to visit him. Service was just beginning at the little oak chapel in the forest. There was the cross-bearer with his small acolytes in red and white; and there were the solitaries in their grey habits and hair girdles. They were chanting a psalm as they went by in procession, and her heart leaped at the sound of Hervé's voice, so that she cried out in her joy: "God's blessing be with you, my dear hermit son. I do not see you, but I would know your voice in a thousand."

It was no great time afterwards that Gourfoed called Hervé to him and said: "To-morrow we fare into the forest, the brethren and I—it may be even so far as the Red Stones, and there shall we rest until my change has come. But my work here in the school I leave to you and your angel. Oh, Hervé, it is better to teach a little child than to work miracles." And when Hervé wrung his hands and was silent for sorrow, the old man put his arms about his shoulders: "Blessed be you, my son, who have lifted my heart up many a day!"

Have you watched the martins "packing" in the red autumn evenings, and seen them racing and winding and crossing in wild glee; and, when they suddenly dropped into the osiers, listened to their multitudinous twittering and chirming in the long willow-beds? That was Hervé's school at work and at play. And the blind teacher was as happy as the children. He contrived curious singing-games for them, and made many simple rhymes which they could easily remember. This was one, which he called

THE RUDDER OR THE ROCK

Little coble,
When the long brown nets are drifting,
And the green waves gently lifting,
Take your ease and have your will.
But when winds are piping shrill,
Heed the rudder!
If you won't obey the rudder,
Then the rock you shall obey.

Another ran like this, and he called it

A SONG OF THINKING

When you waken, let your heart
Of your senses get the start,
Springing up in song and prayer
Higher than the skylark dare.

"Lord, I give Thee," you shall say,
"Here a little child to-day,
Soul and body, wit and will,
Keep him safe from every ill."
See the Fire at work; behold
How he laughs in red and gold!
Think how easily you might
Be as helpful and as bright.

Oh, the heavenly morning Air!
God, like that, is everywhere.
If you rest or if you run,
Think He sees you, like the Sun.

Like the glorious Sun that makes
Roses on the bramble-brakes,
Think He made you, girl and boy,
For His love and for His joy.

When you watch the Carrion-crow
O'er the moorland croaking go,
Think how wickedness must be
Black, and more unclean than he.

And when little Doves unseen
Moan among the tree-tops green,
Think your guardian angels are
Still more sweet, and whiter far.

When the stars begin to peep,
Bless His name before you sleep.
Make a place for Him in bed
Who could nowhere lay His head.

Sign yourself from side to side
With the cross on which He died.
So shall angels' wings be drawn
Round your pillow till the dawn.

Far and wide his songs and sayings were carried, like the winged seeds which the wind sows, till his name was loved in places he would never know; and solitaries came and built their cells near his chapel, that they might live under his rule. The little children grew up and others took their places, and so the years turned until it happened that Hervé was awakened by a cry in the night, and knew that it was his mother calling. He arose and ran out-of-doors, and listened. But all was still in the forest, save for the lightest little wakeful leaves, which whisper Hush, hush! all night long. While he stood in doubt what he should do, some one twitched his habit. He gave a start, but immediately laughed to himself, and, reaching down, felt the shaggy head of Wolf. "Did you too hear? Then we go."

The cocks were crowing and the dogs barking, and they felt the shiver of the new day long before they came to Rivanon. She was lying white and still, at the mercy of God; and it was a world, as they say, to see her face colour and her eyes shine as she embraced her son. Near her was a little maid of six years, and Rivanon took the child's hand and laid it in his: "This is Christina, my niece. She has been with me since her mother died. I give her to you and God." Then in a little while she said under her breath, "O my dear son!" and closed her eyes; and they heard a low sigh of heart's-ease as her angel led her forth.

And now the peace of the forest was vexed by the chiefs of Leon. Ever turbulent and still pagan at heart, they came to Hervé that he might show them the secrets of the stars, and work spells to destroy their enemies; and when he denied them, they harassed him, now with fresh gifts and now with the ruffling of their wild men-at-arms. In his trouble as to whither they should go, he went to ask counsel of Gourfoed, and with him he took Christina and Wolf, for they were his eyes.

They found the great red standing-stones in a distant glade, and in the midst of them the broad slab on four rocks, whereon men had been miserably sacrificed; but all around grew weeds and briars; and half-hidden by these were the ruins of huts, and a low mound marked with a cross of stones. So Hervé knew that the old father Gourfoed was dead, and he returned home sorrowful.

Messengers awaited him from the Bishop of Leon, who would fain have made him a priest, but Hervé was abashed and would not. "Yet, if I be not all unworthy," he said, "ordain me an exorcist, that I may have power against the Evil One." And the good bishop gave him his wish, and counselled him to seek a place of peace in the wilds of Cornouaille, far to the westward.

There they found a sheltered spot, beside a spring in a coombe of the moorland. Ground was granted them, and they cleared and fenced it, and tilled and planted; and built themselves cells, making for Christina a shelter thatched with broom under a cluster of willows. This was her beehive, and Wolf was her guardian and playfellow.

Upon a night when the buckwheat was sprouting, Hervé's sleep was broken with strange dreams. He heard the noise of axe and saw, fall of trees and lopping of boughs, and the sound of mallet and chisel dressing stone. Out of a mist loomed bullock-teams, with timber and grey-green blocks of stone upon the tugs. Men whom he could not see were stacking wood and piling stone in the coombe. Suddenly he was aware of two angels, shining in a great light, and at their feet lay a white scroll. It was unrolled upon the ground, and pebbles lay upon it to keep it open. One angel said to the other, "Shall not Hervé take the chain and help us?" The other answered, "Better that Hervé should first take the scroll and scan it." Then Hervé took up the scroll, and knew it for the builder's plan of a fair minster. One moment he studied the lines and figures; the next he was watching the angels as they marked and measured the ground with the silver chain. All the while the air was humming softly with numberless small voices, as though bees were singing: "Except the Lord—except the Lord shall build the house, they labour in vain—in vain—in vain; except the Lord shall build the house, they labour in vain that build it."

Then out into the unknown land, to manor and farm, to village and town, fared Hervé in quest of all that was needed for the church of his vision. Never before, in the busy streets or on the misty moors, had folk stopped to gaze after such strange wanderers as the blind hermit, bare-headed and bare-footed, with the wolf by his side, and the child flitting like a gleesome elf of the apple-trees. Sometimes they met with but cold comfort, but for the most part their very strangeness won them all they asked for.

When the minster was built it was a world of wonder how anything so beautiful could have been wrought by a blind man; and long afterwards, when aged people told how Hervé used to sing and play to the workmen as they laboured, it became a legend that long ago, on a summer night, the minster had sprung up to the music of an angel.

Who so happy as Christina when Hervé gave her charge of the church, to keep it clean, and to have fair white linen and flowers on the altar? Sometimes when she was singing at her task, he would open the door softly, and stand to listen; but she would hear him, and call, "Uncle, I see you;" and he would quickly steal away, strangely light-hearted.

AND TO HAVE FAIR WHITE LINEN AND FLOWERS ON THE
ALTER.

One stern and thrilling scene entered into Hervé's gentle life before the end. The savage chief Canao had slain his brother Hoel; and setting aside Hoel's little son Judual, had made himself High Prince instead. Treacherous and cruel, he oppressed the people, ravaging their fields and burning their homesteads. Their holy men alone could help them. But when the Bishops of the Nine Churches had warned Canao in vain, they sat in council and found there was but one way to check the tyrant.

They assembled on the solitary hill, Menez-Bré, from which one looks over leagues of country, and along the crinkled shores and the grey sea of Cornouaille. Upon that hill-top was a dolmen of ancient days, and beside it the bishops kindled a torch, and giving it to Hervé, whom they had summoned to them, they bade him utter against Canao the great curse which casts a man forth from all Christian heritage. And Hervé mounted the old stones, and cried the curse abroad, weeping; but instead of extinguishing the torch, as one who dooms a soul to the outer darkness, Hervé laid it upon the rock.

Now, far away, while these things were done upon the hill Menez-Bré, the little Prince Judual fled for safety to the monastery of Leonor. But the holy man, Leonor, knowing how little he was like to be in safety there, sent him down at once to the shore with one of the brethren, and watched anxiously for a sign of their sailing.

Black with rage came Canao, riding from the forest. "Bring me the child," he cried, dismounting. "He is not here," replied Leonor. "Where then?" Leonor pointed to the sea: "Mark yon dark sail upon the waters. He is beneath it, on his way to the King of the Franks."

Canao struck the holy man in the face, and screaming, "Not yet too late!" leaped into the saddle and dashed the spurs into his stallion's flanks. The fierce horse reared with a sharp cry and bounded forward. Hand could not hold him; rein could not turn him. Stones and turf flew from his hoofs as he raced with the bit between his teeth and thundered over the brink of the sea-cliffs.

Far away, upon the hill Menez-Bré, Hervé, instead of extinguishing the torch, laid it upon the rock: "O fathers, let it burn so long as it may, in token of God's mercy!"

The little maid was in her fourteenth year, and it was late in the autumn. The birch-trees glowed in tarnished silver and orange, and berries hung red as blood on the briars. The swallows had flown, and the starlings; and in the bright blustering weather thousands of crumpled leaves flocked and whirled, as if they too would fly.

Christina was singing softly at her work in the church, and Hervé opened the door; but instead of listening, he called her to him: "Christina, little sister, make my bed. Spread it here on the ground before the altar, that I may be at my Saviour's feet. Place a stone for my pillow, and let the bed be ashes, that the Dark Angel may find me lying there."

Christina gazed at him with a frightened face: "Oh, uncle, you are not well. Let me take you away."

"Nay, dear child; but do what I ask, and quickly."

Christina ran, weeping bitterly, and told the brethren; and they, gathering round Hervé, saw that his change was nigh. When the ashes were strewn before the altar, he lay down upon them and said, "Pray for me. My strength is gone; my heart fails; this is the end."

And weeping beside him, Christina prayed: "Oh, uncle, do not leave me. Beg of God to let me follow you quickly, as a little boat follows the stream."

"Beg only, little sister," Hervé answered, "that God's will may be done."

Then Christina went and lay at his feet, clasping them, for they were cold as stone. "How far have I led you, holy feet," she moaned to herself; "and whither will you now go without me?"

For a little time Hervé's lips moved silently. As the Dark Angel stilled them with his touch, the child's heart broke; and turning away from Hervé, the Dark Angel laid his hand tenderly upon her bright hair.

SWORD AND CROSS

IN the eastern valleys of the Biharia Mountains survive the remains of a people unlike any other in Transylvania; once, as they declare, a powerful race and lords of all the land north of the bright windings of the River Maros. They live in quaint villages which retain the shape of the old waggon laagers of their ancestors. On a grassy mound in the open space within the village stands the timber church, with its green spire and red walls. They have a breed of dogs, brought from their ancient home in the East, and these are not to be matched for strength, speed, and intelligence.

Although they are good Christians, strange beliefs and traditions of a far-off time are mingled with their creed; and the most curious token of this is the cross they preserve in the oldest of their churches as a copy of the first cross venerated by their forefathers. It is of great age and of a singular form. Instead of a figure of the Redeemer, a sword, the hilt and cross-bar of which are banded with gold and roughly set with garnets and topazes of many colours, is sunk into the wood, and held in its place with strips of silver.

The old travellers have made many guesses as to the meaning of the cross inlaid with the jewelled sword; this is its story.

When Kunda, the King of the Urogs, was very old he dreamed a dream; and he called together his warrior chiefs and the priests and magicians. Armed with bow and lance, net and whip, they gathered about him on their horses, as was their custom, and hoary and nearly blind with years, he sat in the midst of them on his saddle and told his dream.

"Speak to the children of the Sword," he said, "and bid them make ready for long wanderings. We are called hence into the ways of the setting sun. For in my sleep I heard the cry of the Sword, and this was the cry: 'Open thine eyes and watch whither I go. Thither, too, shall my children go, roaming far, fighting often, resting little, till I shall bring them into the land which I shall win for them.' Yea, and I beheld the Sword. It was brandished before me as by a mighty hand unseen: and as I watched, it travelled across the rolling steppes, through swamps and forests, over sweeping rivers, and once through the midst of a vast water. At sunrise the blade and the jewels glittered with light; at nightfall, when the sun went down beyond it, its shadow stretched across the world to my feet. Sometimes the unseen hand bore it lightly, but often it seemed to hew its way as it went. Far away it climbed through rocks and trees to the chine of high mountains. There its point was lowered and waved right and left, and as I looked down from the mountains this was the cry of the Sword: 'This is the land. Speak to my children and bid them come and take possession.' Then the hand brandished the blade aloft, fixed it in the rock by the hilt, snatched it up again, and planted it point downwards."

And the old king, gazing round on these wild, eager-eyed nomads who had seen but the sandy deserts sprinkled with thorns, and the marshy shores of the Caspian, and the illimitable steppes which turned to a dull brown when the spring rains had ceased, told of a land more rich and beautiful than it seemed possible for the world to contain—a land of shadows as well as of sun, of game as well as of pasture, where hunger and thirst were unknown. "But why the Sword was first planted point upwards and then reversed, that," he said, "I know not."

All that year the tribes prepared for their emigration, and in the following spring, when the grasses flowered shoulder-high on the wide prairies, a mighty multitude gathered for their exodus; the women and children in numberless ox-waggons, the men on the swift little horses from which they seemed to be inseparable.

Before they set out, the great Sword which they worshipped was unwound from its silk wrappings and reared upon the mound of sacrifice. The priests chanted their savage hymn of the red death. Seven men, captured in a raid undertaken for the sacrifice, were led forth, and one by one the priests slew them with the Sword. While the victims fell and the idol was again planted, with its hilt buried in the turf to the jewelled cross-bar, and the blade reddened with slaughter, the barbaric chant rose once more from the mound:

> "Drink thy seven-fold cup, thou glittering god!
> With treasure we have decked thee,
> Fair of colour is thy raiment;
> Drink, shining hero, and quench thy thirst!
> What sons hast thou to avenge thee?
> None, if we are not thy sons.
> What brides hast thou?
> Our women are thy brides.
> Be ever gracious and victorious,
> Lest our worship be turned to a song of reviling;
> March mightily before us,
> Lest we leave thee wifeless and childless."

Twice during that long journey the tall grasses of the steppes were burnt up in the blaze of summer, and twice the winter beat with snow and hail on their waggon-laager. Spaces strewn with whitened bones marked for many a year where they stood and fought and conquered and pushed on again to the country of the vision. For centuries afterwards shepherds watched their flocks on the vast plains from the tops of the mounds in which they laid their great warriors fallen; the little heaps which covered those who had sickened and died by the way were but as waves of the mid sea, visible for a moment and then lost for ever in the waste.

Following a hunted stag, they forded the shallows of the Sea of Azov; how they carried their long team of waggons over the broad rivers of the West is still an unexplained wonder.

In the third springtime they came to the mountain forests and ascended to the blue summits from which Kunda had seen the Sword pointing downwards and waving right and left over the inheritance of the Urogs.

The aged king looked down from the top of the pass, but to his dim eyes all below was a vague brightness. "Is it indeed," he asked, "a fair land of sun and shadow? Was the cry of the Sword a song of truth?"

"No fairer land have I ever beheld," replied Zagon the high priest.

It was that Dacia beyond Danube and the deep woods which Trajan had conquered, and which the Romans had abandoned to the barbarians over a hundred years. The great roads still traversed it, reaching out into infinite distance; and these silent highways which had overawed the northern invaders were now to fill the Urogs with more amazement than the ruined temples and the forsaken cities. Large trees had spread their branches over the old camps; a darker growth of legends—wild stories of phantoms and deadly hoards of treasure arose around the grass-grown streets and pillared forums; and the spell of these mysterious remains was to fall upon the newcomers.

"Over all," said Zagon, "there is a dazzle of gold; green and wide are the pastures; strange encampments too, I see—folk, doubtless, who dwell in tents and laagers of stone, such as those we slew on the plains."

"Then peace be on thy head, O Sword, thou glittering god of the world!" cried Kunda; "Now I have lived long enough." And as the hoary man spoke he sank forward on his horse's neck.

When they raised him up they found that he was dead. His son Haba was chosen in his place, and bearing the old king with them they poured down the mountains into the land which the Sword had promised.

That sudden invasion brought Goths and Getes face to face with an enemy more fierce and ruthless even than themselves. The swarms of horsemen scattered and wheeled and dashed round them like a scurry of clouds in a tempest. They charged in a flight of arrows or a rush of spears. If the Goths broke and fled, trained packs of dogs, half-wolf, with spiked collars, pursued them and pulled them down. Did a champion shake his long yellow hair and stride out for single combat, a net was flung over him and he was cut down amid shrieks of laughter. Even within the trenches death hovered over the camp fires, for the archers of the night were abroad, and every gleam of flame was a mark for, an arrow. And upon the town walls the defenders learned to be wary, for as a troop of flying horsemen swept past, one would ride nearer and suddenly swing his whip round his head; a slender thong would flash like a living thing over a space of thirty feet and curl about the neck of a man-at-arms, and in an instant the hapless wretch would be plucked from the battlements. Night was haunted by a new terror for the scouts. Steal as craftily as they might through the darkness, they came upon the Ugor—the man asleep in his saddle, the horse alert and watchful; and the snapping of dry wood or the tread of a careless foot awakened a hoarse cry and brought a score of shadowy riders to the spot. People began to believe that these terrible rovers lived, ate, slept, died on horseback; indeed it was said at last that the Ugor was a beast-man, the evil and mysterious offspring of the desert.

As the invaders moved westwards through the fruitful land, they came to Ravna, a little walled town built out of the wreck of a Roman city on one of the great roads. Fragments of marble columns still lay half-buried on the green mounds which covered the ruins; and for some distance on each side the highway was lined with the stately tombs of the vanished Romans. Many of these structures had fallen into decay; the largest had been rifled for treasure, the sculptured marble coffins had been broken open, and the ashes of the dead cast out to the four winds.

In one of these chambers of silence the saintly Eirenion had taken up his abode. For many years he had wandered over Dacia, proclaiming the tidings of salvation. Disciples had gathered about his hermitage; he had taught them and sent them abroad to the towns and villages. The common people adored him; even the proudest of the Gothic warriors treated him with reverence. It was never forgotten how, long ago, the great Bishop Wulfila, after blessing his labours and embracing him with the kiss of peace, had turned to the chiefs and said in a low voice: "Bow down your heads before this man. Ask not his name, but know that once, under Constantine the Emperor, he was a greater soldier than any of you, and to-day he is the beloved servant of the Lord Christ." In his grey hair and his humble garb he stood now as tall and commanding as they, and folk still talked of the time when he was a leader of the legions.

Now it befell in these days of warfare with the Ugors that as Eirenion knelt in his hermitage praying for the peace and welfare of his people, he was startled by a long sound of moaning, which grew into a clamour of voices and the noise of a multitude in rapid movement. Going to the entrance of the tomb, he saw that it was a host of men fleeing in mad rout to the town for safety.

The ranks of the Goths had been broken and panic had fallen upon their host. He hastened to the roadside and stretching his hands up against them, he cried in a loud voice, "Turn, men, and make a stand!" But the crowds rushed on, panting and shouting, with white, wet faces. Many broke away at his cry and dispersed among the tombs and the mounds of the Roman ruins, but in the blindness of fear hundreds were swept past the town gates, and were conscious only of the long straight road before them.

As the confused mass streamed along, Eirenion perceived that the swarthy horsemen, here and there in twos and threes, here and there in sixes and sevens, were mingled with the yellow-haired fugitives; and as they rode, their arrows flew before them, lances were plunged forward and downwards with rapid thrusts, swords flashed right and left; and ever the heaving and shouting chaos raced on until the rout closed in the dense swarms of the Ugor horde.

During the fruitless attack upon the town, the fighting among the tombs, and the fierce pursuit on the long, straight road, Eirenion ministered to the wounded and the dying. When the first skirmishers showed that the enemy were returning he stood a little aside to scan the appearance of these unknown wanderers. Now and again horsemen started out from the savage throng, threatening to ride him down; they saw the tall priest erect, with kingly eyes, wave his hand in a great sign of the cross between him and them, and they fell back awe-struck.

In the midst of the horde appeared a band of prisoners on foot, blood-stained and bound with thongs. Eirenion moved towards them with a friendly gesture, and was allowed to take his place at their head. "Whither you go, sons," he cried, "I go with you, if it be God's will. Let us fare onwards without care, trusting in Him, the Most Mighty. In His hands is the gift of life, in His hands is the gift of death, and which gift is the better for us He alone knoweth. Remember the strong hearts of your fathers even in the days when they knew Him not, and quit you as true men of Christ."

And continually, as they marched on, he raised his voice in hymns and prayers, so that the Ugors looked on with amazement, and called to each other, "This man is their mighty magician. See how proudly now these slaves go, and how he has made their faces to shine!"

Wounded and weary, they lay that night under the stars with the trained dogs couched in a circle round them; and a single sentry, slumbering on his horse, was their only human guard. Never was the light of the sun more sweet to men's eyes than that which warmed them on the morrow. Then as the noise and stir of the day began, the Ugor priests came and surveyed the captives, and choosing seven of the youngest and comeliest they led them away.

Eirenion went forth with them. Passing through a throng of horsemen, they came to a mound in the midst of the encampment, and as Eirenion looked up and saw, fixed on the summit of the mound, a naked sword which glittered, "This sword," he said, "is surely the idol of these heathen people, and they will slay these men as an offering. Lord God, let not this be!"

Eagerly he glanced about for king or leader in that strange horde. A little apart stood two men who seemed more commanding than the rest, and hastening towards them he addressed them in words and in gestures so expressive that most of what he said was as clear as though he had spoken in their own tongue:

"These men are worshippers of that Almighty One in the heavens who is the Lord and Giver of life. He hath made them in His image; their blood you shall not shed to the idol of your people. He of you who is king, let him take his sword and free them from their bonds."

"Behold, Zagon," said Haba, "this man is a priest of great power even as thou art thyself. He would unbind the victims. Let it be as he says. They cannot escape the Sword."

The priest frowned, but he went and cut their thongs, and the captives made no movement, but stood in their place watching Eirenion.

Then pointing to the naked sword on the mound, Eirenion said to the king, "Cast down this idol of slaughter and of sorrow, and turn thy heart to the true God who takes no delight in the shedding of blood." And even while Eirenion was speaking he was vaguely aware of the words of the Evangelist, "Not to send peace but a sword," the jewelled cross-bar seemed to flash light into his very soul, and suddenly he perceived how in shape and in meaning Sword and Cross were one. He drew from his breast a silver cross, and put it into Haba's hands:

"Look, King, upon this sign and upon that. Let me show thee how thou and thy people shall bow down and worship."

BEHOLD, YE PEOPLE, THE SIGN OF OUR REDEEMING.

Swiftly he sprang up the mound, plucked the weapon from the turf, and brandished it with a joyful shout. "Behold, ye people, the sign of our redeeming," and planting it point downwards in the earth—no longer a murderous Sword but a glorious Cross—knelt with bowed head before it.

The daring act was greeted with a tumultuous uproar, but Haba lifted his hand for silence. "Sons of the Sword," he cried, "this too was in the vision of Kunda my father. Did ye not hear him say that the hand of the Spirit of the Sword first fixed it by the hilt, then snatched it up, and planted it with its point in the rock? This man, whoever he may be, is truly some priest of strange power, and has wrought as the Spirit of the Sword bade him. Behold now, and heed it well, he is Haba's friend."

Eirenion descended from the mound, and taking the silver cross he showed the king how it resembled the reversed weapon which they had so barbarously adored. He strove to tell him how the Son of God had come down from heaven and died a cruel death for the sins of men, but Haba, though he listened gravely, could understand but little of what was said of the mystery of redemption.

After the captive Goths had been set free, Eirenion remained and took up his abode with the Ugors; and as though he had received some portion of the divine gift of tongues he quickly mastered their language. With undying patience he taught them, winning their wild hearts to gentleness and peace; and many thousands were baptised in the waters of the Dacian streams.

He explained to them the mystery of the corn-fields, how they nourished the world, and the craft of fire and the craft of water, so that they should rise to a higher life than that of the beast which slays and devours and has no store or comfort against the hard winter. Purging their gross worship, yet taking thought of the way in which men cling to the customs of their fathers, he wrought for them a symbol which blended together both Cross and Sword; and wreathing this with the branches of trees in the months of blossom, and with fair fruit and ears of corn in. the harvest, they offered a bloodless sacrifice.

Most of the Ugor priests furiously resisted these changes; and the more savage spirits of the horde, revolting from Haba and taking Zagon for king, drew a great following after them as they swept away westwards. A little time after that, when the Huns burst in myriads over the mountains, these tribes threw in their lot with the invaders.

But Eirenion made peace between his converts and the Goths and Getes, and Haba led them into the valleys of the Biharia mountains, where they outlived the nomad hunger for constant change and the vast, free spaces of the desert and the steppes. Eirenion died among them in extreme old age; and the humble priest who had been one of the great soldiers of Constantine was laid by these sons of the Cross and Sword in such a mound as they had been used to raise over the mightiest of their warriors.

THE SOUL OF JUSTINIAN

IT was the festival of the Star, the Star of the Magi. An unclouded sun glittered on the waters of the Golden Horn, on the swift ocean-stream which divided the eastern from the western world, on the beauty and splendour of Constantinople.

The vast Hippodrome was thronged, and the marble benches glowed like a hanging garden with the colours of the rival factions of the city, the Blues and Greens, and their allies the Reds and Whites. The confused noise of upwards of thirty thousand people swelled into a long indescribable roar as the flying chariots, gay with party colours, dashed down the course in a storm of thundering hoofs and tossing manes, doubled round the goal-pillar, and swept back again on the further side of the statues and obelisks which filled the long central space of the stadium.

With a somewhat moody aspect Justinian surveyed the stirring spectacle from his throne. Every now and again as some fresh demonstration drew his attention to the Greens, his eyes rested on their ranks in cold displeasure. Almost from the beginning this faction had disturbed the games with their persistent outcries: "Health to Cæsar! Long life to Cæsar! Listen to the oppressed; grant us justice!" Race after race their complaint rose in shriller clamour against the Quæstor Tribonian and the Prefect John of Cappadocia, who were filling their own coffers by their merciless extortions. "We are poor, we are ground down, we are fleeced and flayed. If we must die, let it be in thy service. Victory to Cæsar!"

At the twentieth race Justinian lost patience. He made a sign to one of his heralds, and a ringing voice carried the imperial rebuke over the wide expanse of the amphitheatre: "Peace, you mouths of brass! Silence and humility, you thankless Jews and Samaritans!" The cries of the faction became but the more vehement, and as the herald flung back the accents of the emperor's irritation and scornful indifference, the appeals for justice and relief turned into howls of rage and vituperation: "We renounce thee, Cæsar! Justinian without justice! Cursed be the day this man's father was born! Thracian tyrant and protector of thieves!"

The emperor himself rose grimly from his throne, and for a moment dead silence fell upon the multitude. "Have you no care for your lives?" he asked in cold, clear tones which travelled far.

It was the thoughtless folly of an angry man. The words were taken as an incentive by the Blues, whom Justinian had hitherto generally favoured. The faction, loyalist in politics and orthodox in faith, included the wild and lawless youth of the city, who affected the long hair and ruffling garb of the Barbarians, went secretly armed by day and infested the streets at night.

They sprang down from their seats, and in an instant the course of the Hippodrome was filled with yelling crowds mingled in savage conflict. The Greens, overborne by their opponents, turned and fled, and for hours the streets of Constantinople were given over to riot and bloodshed. Seven of the ringleaders of both parties were captured by the police, summarily tried, condemned, and hurried off to execution. Five were beheaded; the ropes broke as the last two—a Blue and a Green—were being hanged, and the mob overwhelmed the guard and rescued them.

For the time being the factions set aside their mutual hatred, and made common cause against the tyrant who oppressed his people and the patron who assassinated his adherents. The prisons were emptied, palaces and private mansions pillaged, and at the first attempt of the civic troops to quell the sedition, the city was set on fire. In the spreading flames, which threatened to reduce the capital of the East to ashes, perished amid the wreck of priceless works of antiquity and the loss of enormous treasure the noble Cathedral of Sancta Sophia, founded by Constantine.

For five days the destinies of the Empire trembled in the scales. The factions chose another Cæsar, and crowned him in the Hippodrome with a woman's necklace. In the palace Justinian, disheartened and unnerved, took counsel with his chief ministers and the officers of his guard whether, like the Emperor Zeno, he should seek refuge for a time in Asia. John the Cappadocian and most of his colleagues gave their voice for flight.

Beyond the blue strait of the Bosporus the sunny shores lay within view. Already this disastrous course seemed to have been adopted, when the future of the world was decided by the fairest and the proudest woman in Europe.

"A woman's voice," said the Empress Theodora, "is an unwelcome sound in the council chamber; but those who have most at stake have the best right to speak. Death is the common lot of sovereign and slave; but flight from death is the coward's choice. Even if flight meant safety, I should not flee. Not for one hour shall I forego this diadem or yield the name of empress. Yonder is the sea; there are the ships. Escape is easy. But consider, Cæsar! When you have bartered empire for the bread of exile and honour for safety, will desire to live ensure you against an ignoble end? For my part I am at one with the old saying: The purple robe is a brave shroud."

Fired by her intrepid spirit, Justinian sprang to his feet: "No more talk of retreat; here we hold to the end!"

"You need a man," said Theodora; "Belisar is here."

The emperor inclined with a gracious smile to the tall figure of the brilliant young Thracian, just returned from the Persian war. "What troops have you, General?"

"Five hundred horse, Cæsar, and some two thousand Veterans."

"Then trample me out these factious firebrands."

Rumours of Justinian's flight had spread through Constantinople, and the success of the revolution appeared already secured. The insurgents crowded the Hippodrome, hailing their necklace Cæsar with cries of "Long life and victory." An attempt to take them by surprise through the winding staircase between the palace and the amphitheatre was found to be impracticable; and Belisar, dividing his forces, assailed at the same moment the two main portals. As he forced his way through the Gate of Death, he gazed with the pity of a great soldier on the immense multitude. At the startling apparition of the cavalry and the imperial standard, the people rose in masses and rushed down headlong into the clearest course; the trumpets sounded; the issues were choked by the crush of struggling fugitives; the terrible carnage began.

The slain were counted by tens of thousands, and for a generation the cries and colours of the factions were unknown in the streets of the capital.

In his calmer moments Justinian too regretted that horrible destruction of men whom God had made in His own image. One taunt hurled at him by the Greens rankled in his memory—"Justinian the Unjust!" His Thracian name, his name as a shepherd lad on the green plains about Sardica, had been Uprauda, the Upright. He had been raised from the sheepfold to the throne, and he was smitten with remorse as he reflected how the neglect of justice, the refusal to right the wrong, had brought about the catastrophe.

And the great church, the church of the Divine Wisdom, the Eternal Word, the Second Person of the Holy Trinity, had gone up in flames through his folly. Henceforth his twofold purpose in life should be to raise a temple beyond the dreams of human worship, and to reunite the East and the West in one world-empire under the cross of Christ.

Justinian slept but little. Rising early, he devoted the day to affairs of state; after sunset his own day began. He read and wrote far into the night, wandered for hours through the dim corridors, or mused in the moonlight or under the brilliant stars on the long marble galleries which overlooked the gardens and the sea.

The blackened heaps of the ruined cathedral had not yet been wholly cleared away when, upon one of those spring-like nights which occur in January, the emperor, as he paced the outer gallery, became conscious of an extraordinary brightness in the air and a marvellous clearness of vision. Far away beyond the silvery waters of the Propontis—far away and yet so vivid as to seem near—he beheld the lofty white pillars of an old temple on a wooded hill in a green island. The temple was in ruins; most of the great columns had been shaken down by earthquake, but those which were still standing gleamed with strange beauty in the wonderful luminousness of the night.

Was Justinian dreaming, or was this a vision granted to the eyes of the spirit?

"Thus in the days of that ignorance at which God winked—"

The words were spoken close by his side. Startled, he turned and glanced around, but he was alone on the starlit gallery; and the low crystalline voice, which seemed to come out of the air, continued:

"Thus it was that people worshipped aforetime what they believed to be divine, for unto no man hath been denied some inkling of Him who breathed the spirit of life into the clay He fashioned. Yon isle is Cyzicus; the temple was that of Cybele, whom men adored as the venerable mother of the gods. Look further!"

In the warm hush and magical transparency of the night there appeared to glide before him, not a picture, but the living aspect of the idolatry of the pagan world.

"The white city between the hillsides and the harbour," said the voice, "is Ephesus. The clamour of the silversmiths has long been laid with dust; Diana the Great has fallen; yet these mighty columns of green jasper still flash out over the sea to the passing ships. Delos thou knowest, this little isle of the Cyclades, 'the star of the dark earth.' Here between the cedars and the snow, in the valley between the mountains, behold the City of the Sun and the thousand pillars of the shrine of Osiris. Why art thou moved? Why do thine eyes fill with light? What thought has sprung up in thy heart?"

"Lord God," cried Justinian, raising his hands in ecstasy, "Let me live to build a new house to thy glory. Let the dead praise Thee whom they knew not when they were alive. Let the ancient worship of all lands add its splendour to the splendour of Thy temple. Shall not the great and costly stones which men reared to Isis and Cybele and all their shadowy dreams of Thee rear Thy cross into the heavens? So suffer Thy name to be uplifted high above all names, and the revelation of Thy mercy to be exalted over all that the world has believed and hoped of Thee!"

"Then let me help thee," said the voice. He felt a touch upon his shoulder, as light as a snowflake. Beside him stood an angel, six-winged, dimly luminous, scarcely separable from the air, yet softly iridescent with the innumerable colours of gems and flowers.

"Look, does this please thee?"

With a thrill of rapture Justinian beheld on the palm of the angel's hand the model of such a church as had never yet been conceived by human genius. Without and within he saw it, with its storied walls and springing columns, from the golden pavement to the glittering dome, which floated airily aloft as though it were hung from a starry chain.

"LOOK AGAIN AND YET AGAIN", SAID THE ANGEL.

"Look again and yet again," said the angel, "so that thou shalt not forget anything thou hast been shown."

"Give me angels to achieve this," said the emperor; "it is a labour and a glory beyond the skill and strength of men."

"Then thou couldst scarcely say the work was thine. Nay, come thou but as near as thou canst to the vision which has been vouchsafed thee. Therein man touches the topmost flower of service."

"Stay yet a moment," cried Justinian, as the angelic form began to fade away into the starlit air. But only the low clear voice answered from lips unseen, "God prosper thee with all happiness," and the emperor was alone.

Early on the morrow he summoned the famous architects, Anthemius the Lydian and Isidore of Miletus; and laying before them rude drawings of the great basilica, he described the wondrous church which he had seen in the angel's hand. As they listened, they referred from time to time to his drawings, and rapidly sketched plans of the edifice which his words conjured up in the mind's eye. Noting each stroke of their pencils and answering the questions they asked, Justinian corrected and changed many of the lines of their draughting. "Not so," he would say; "but thus it was and thus."

Then he told them how their labour would be lightened and shortened by the store of wrought marble and costly stone brought from other lands. "Time is fleeting, flesh fades as the flower-de-luce, life flutters to its fall as the leaf on the tree; wherefore, I pray you, make good speed. Treasure shall not fail. Material you shall not lack, nor men. A hundred master-builders you shall have, and each master-builder a hundred workmen; and I would have five thousand labouring on the right hand, and five thousand on the left, and daily at sundown each shall be paid in silver pieces."

Think now that you see the enormous task begun; that as if by enchantment the past is again alive, and stirring and resounding with the din of traffic and labour. On the cleared ground the masters measure off with white wands ten times the area of Solomon's Temple. Hundreds of men dig in the trenches; hundreds plant deep the foundation courses. The slaking lime fumes in white pools among the tawny sand-heaps. The huge scaffold poles are lashed together.

In the distant brick-fields swarms of people hurry to and fro; bricks dry in long streets; the kilns smoke like a plundered city. War-galleys and broad-beamed merchant ships heave in from the freshening sea with slabs and drums from the granite and porphyry quarries and the sculptured spoils of the vanished gods. The sailors pull together to their wild sea-chants; the giant cranes swing their burdens round; teams of huge-horned cattle and gangs of half-naked slaves strain at the hawsers, and the rollers groan under the colossal loads.

Day after day, clad in coarse linen tunic and white headcloth, with a plain staff in his hand, Justinian mingled with the ten thousand workmen whose lowly lives were being wrought into the vast structure of the basilica. Penetrating everywhere, noting everything, climbing from scaffold to scaffold, putting a royal hand to some effort of strength, he passed from one busy group to another, praised, scolded, encouraged, jested, rewarded pieces of rapid and skilful labour with extraordinary gifts.

With flushed cheeks and radiant eyes he gazed at last at the magnificent columns which towered above him. East and west of the massive piers which were to heave the dome into the blue heavens, eight porphyry pillars, based on white marble, crowned with white marble, recalled the splendour of the temple of the Sun. "O Diana of the Ephesians," he exclaimed, "these on the north and south were of thy treasures of green jasper, larger and more beautiful than any! These were thine, O Virgin Pallas, when men adored thee at Athens; these thine, O Phœbus, the Shining Archer, when they worshipped thee in Delos; these thine, venerable mother of the gods, in the morning of time at Cyzicus. Now, Lord, are they all Thine, glory to Thee and to Thy Christ!"

Nor were Justinian's the only eyes which ranged watchfully over the work of the great church. When the masons were finishing the eastern niche, shaped like a vast sea-shell, wherein the altar was to stand, there was much questioning as to how the light should fall upon it. The architects had planned for but one window, but Justinian said, "Nay, surely, let there be two."

Then said Anthemius the Lydian, bowing low: "Will not Cæsar take account of the imagery and significance which may beautify these things? One is the true light which enlighteneth every man. There is one altar and one sacrifice. One faith there is and one baptism; one fold and one shepherd; one God and Father of all."

"Yea, Cæsar," added Isidore of Miletus, "and doth not Ecclesiastes say, 'There is one alone, and there is not a second'?"

The emperor laughed outright: "And verily Ecclesiastes also saith, 'Two are better than one,' and I would bid thee remember, Anthemius, that God made two great lights; two ways there are whereon men shall tremble grievously in the dark, and these are Life and Death; two movements are there of the reason and will whereon man stands in sore need of illumination, and these are Yea and Nay. And whether these be good reasons or not, methinks more light will fall on the altar from two windows than from one."

"Let the light come from three windows, and this shall be the altar of the Holy Trinity!"

The words were uttered by a tall man of great beauty and majesty. He came towards them as he spoke. They observed with surprise that he was clothed in purple, and that his shoes were of the same imperial colour. For a moment his eyes turned from one to the other, then with a bewildering suddenness he vanished from their sight.

Not many days later, when all the place was still at the hour of the noontide slumber, and a little lad watched the masons' tools, there came a stately man in brilliant white robes. This, thought the lad, is doubtless the chief eunuch or some high officer of the palace, and he bowed low to him.

"Go, child, and waken the men," said the stranger, "and bid them return to their labour. The hour of sleep is gone by."

"Is this the order of Cæsar, lord?"

"It is my bidding."

"Then I dare not, great lord, they would slay me ere they were well awake."

"Then get thee to the emperor, and bid him come to me."

"This is my place, illustrious one," the lad answered, "here I watch the tools and keep all safe; and though I would readily serve thee, from this spot I must not budge."

"I will watch and guard for thee."

The lad looked up full of doubt and shook his head. "A lost life should I be were I to go hence, and the men were to find the place untended."

"Nay, then, unbeliever, I vow by the Holy Wisdom not to quit this spot, but to keep all safe till thy return. Do as I bid thee."

Then the lad ran upon his errand, and as he drew near the palace, he met the emperor coming forth in his workman's garb. Having fallen at his feet, he looked up and panted: "I was sent to thee, Lord of the World: have I leave to speak?"

"Speak," said Justinian; and when the lad had told his story, "Think a little," he said, "and be very sure of what thou sayest. Were those the very words he spoke? Repeat them."

The lad repeated them: "I vow by the Holy Wisdom not to quit this spot but to keep all safe till thy return."

Then joyfully laughed Justinian: "Of such a guardian never could I have dreamed. Now may I ask trustfully, Watchman, what of the night? Watchman, what of the dawn? Come, boy, with me."

He hastened back to the palace. To one high officer he said: "Have a ship ready to sail at once for the Cyclades." To another: "Give the child meat and drink and raiment. When the ship is ready put him aboard, and stay on the wharf till thou canst see it no longer." To a third: "Seek out the lad's home, and provide for his family if they would depart with him." To the lad himself: "Henceforth I will see to thy welfare, but never more do thou return to Constantinople."

Lo! now, with an easy heart Justinian watched the cupolas and the vast dome arise. The vaulting was in white tiles of Rhodian clay, marvellous for lightness. On the tiles was graven:

> "God hath founded it; overthrown it shall not be;
> He will uphold it in the blush of dawn;"

and the masons, as they set them, built in sacred relics, and hymns were sung in the nave far below. Four-and-twenty windows seemed to lift the dome clear into the air. From its inner surface looked down four six-winged seraphs, wrought in little cubes of gilt glass and glittering colours. The dazzle of the gold cross that crowned it without was seen in Bithynia from the snowy tops of Olympus.

Then were all the walls covered with the beauty of marble—slabs of purple Phrygian with silver stars, of green Laconian, of blue Lybian, of black Celtic with white veins, of pale Lydian with red flowers. But wearisome would it be to tell of all the splendour of silver and bronze, of ivory and amber, of cedar and chrysoprase. Neither will I speak of the altar shimmering with gems as the Milky Way shimmers with stars, nor of the four-and-twenty colossal books of the Gospels, bound in thick plates of gold. More peaceful and sweet it is to think of the cool pavement, in which the marble was marked as with the ripples of waters flowing in four rivers through Paradise; and of the baptismal font, which was a copy of the well whereon Jesus sat, wearied in Samaria.

Five years, eleven months, and ten days after its foundation the church of the Holy Wisdom was consecrated. The year was the year of our Lord 538, and the day was Christmas Eve.

Justinian drove from the palace, like a victor in a chariot drawn by four horses. The Patriarch received him at the lofty portals. Over the entrance the Bible upon a throne was figured in a bas-relief of bronze, and upon its open page was written: "I am the door; by me if any man enter in—" Justinian ran from the threshold to the stately terraced rostrum, and there he said, with arms outstretched: "Praised be the Lord God, who hath deemed me worthy to achieve such a work. Solomon, I have surpassed thee!"

So Justinian had his heart's desire.

From the pinnacles of greatness the Thracian shepherd lad Uprauda looked out abroad over the nations, dreaming of his world-empire. Under the suns of three continents, Belisar, who had already saved him, fought his battles, ever loyal and irresistible. Conquest was added to conquest; tribute and spoil was poured into his treasury; kings clad in purple were led in triumph through the streets to his footstool crying, "Vanity, vanity! all is vanity!"

In the watches of the night, as he wandered with sleepless energy, he was tempted to challenge the mighty seraph who kept watch and ward, faithful to his vow, in the shadows of Sancta Sophia. And behold! as often as that thought was played with in the emperor's fancy the angel heard it sounding down the nave like the challenge of the guards on the city walls in the dark.

With the wondrous vision of angelic beings the seraph saw into Justinian's soul, and breathed a long sigh: "How quickly the small seeds of evil spring! A little time ago thou saidst in thy thoughtlessness, 'God hath deemed me worthy!' Then came vanity crying from thy lips, 'Solomon, I have surpassed thee!' Then thou didst glory in thy reforms of justice, 'Bow down, world, and obey my law.' To-day thou wouldst jest with a spirit who stands before the Throne. Vainglorious fool! To-morrow thou wilt make thyself God's vicegerent—nay, I will look no more!—thou sinkest from baseness to baseness!"

As the seraph foresaw, so it happened. Justinian snatched the keys of Peter. What he proclaimed, that should the Universal Church believe. None should gainsay him. The Pope Vigilius was seized and carried to Constantinople. Armed men invaded the sanctuary and tore him by the beard from the altar. Imprisoned, excommunicated by the emperor's orders, his name blotted from the tablets of the churches, the old man was at last suffered to depart, and died of sorrow and bodily anguish on his way to Rome. The Patriarch Eutychius was banished, and driven from monastery to monastery.

More ignoble still was his treatment of Belisar. Jealousy and envy embittered him against the fearless soldier whom he had once honoured with the only triumph granted to a subject in the course of four hundred years. The one man, to whom he owed sovereignty and perhaps life itself, was received with coldness, dogged with suspicion, ignominiously recalled from his commands. His veteran bodyguard was disbanded; half his wealth confiscated. Distrusted and feared, he was still indispensable, and once and again, saddened but unrepining, the strong man was ready at his master's need.

After the death of the empress deep gloom, full of cares and disquietudes, fell upon Justinian, and with the advance of age he was seized with an insatiable avarice. Already oppressed with taxation for the defence of the empire, the people groaned under their new burdens. And now, in spite of his chains of fortresses, the Huns crossed the Danube, poured through the Balkan passes, and ravaged the Thrace of his boyhood. One flying horde of four thousand horse dashed up to the very towers of Constantinople. A cry for Belisar went up from the trembling city.

For the last time the old warrior buckled on the harness of the victor days. The only troops on which he could depend were three hundred of his veteran guards. Half-armed peasants, crowds of untrained citizens gave a show of strength. Clouds of dust, numberless fires disheartened the enemy. As the barbaric squadrons advanced to the onset, they were shaken by the clamour of a host rushing in on all sides from the woods. They were taken in front and flank. The hero and his guards hewed down the foremost; the rest broke and fled in a hopeless rabble.

The capital was saved. Cheering crowds escorted Belisar to the palace. The courtiers were silent. With a frigid embrace the emperor thanked and dismissed him.

Envy and distrust and malice tracked the old lion-heart to the end. He was charged with plotting against the emperor. Justinian spared his life, but stripped him of his honours and estate.

"For five-and-thirty years," said the hero, lifting his proud head, "I have been thy true liegeman. Look in my face, Cæsar; is it the face of a traitor?"

"Many faces are masks," replied Justinian gloomily.

"No mask wholly covers falsehood, Cæsar. As the soul of a man is, such is his face."

"I will speak with thee again," said Justinian, and turning away he muttered to himself, "Faces, faces! As I sit in the dusk they come upon me in multitudes—street-throngs, swarms of the Hippodrome. I had never thought people had so many different faces. They pass me by in crowds; peaceful, angry; idle, busy; merry, full of care. Some turn to me but do not see me. Women look into my eyes—so many women; dark and radiant, laughing girls, icy patricians. Some speak to me breathlessly. I hear the sound of their voices, but the words I cannot hear. And each of these, he would say, is the mirror of the soul. Let me consider this!"

Now in the last year of the emperor's reign a letter was found in Sancta Sophia on the massive silver chair in which he used to sit. Justinian opened it and read:

"Eutychius to Justinian. From the cloister in Amesea. The Lord hath spoken to me and I am troubled on thy account. Think of thy vainglory; think of thy presumption; think of thy sacrileges; think of thy cruelty; think of thy avarice; think of thy ingratitude. They are written in the Everlasting Book. Thy people curse thee. Across thy empire is written, *Mene, Mene, Tekel, Upharsin.*

Think of thy days, which are numbered. I pray for thee."

The heart of the emperor was hot with wrath. As he paced through the long moonlit corridors that night—for though he was now a man four score years and over, his spirit was yet more sleepless and untiring than of old—he crumpled the Patriarch's letter in his hand, saying below his breath, "Surely, surely, I will slay this man."

A belated courtier, hurrying through the corridor, beheld him standing in a space of bright moonlight. Justinian's back was towards him, but he knew the rich robes and tall figure of the emperor, and approached with profound obeisances. At the sound of footsteps Justinian turned and spoke. The courtier gazed, grew white and trembled, rubbed his eyes, looked again, and then fled with a roar of horror. Lord God, where is his face?"

In garb and presence it was the emperor; the jewelled circlet gleamed in his shaggy white hair; but to the emperor's head there was no face.

As the rushing footsteps echoed along the marble walls, the great six-winged angel appeared at Justinian's side. The emperor's heart was stricken with dismay.

"How is it thou art here?" he cried. "Hast thou forgotten thy charge in the great church? Didst thou not vow to watch and ward—"

"Till the lad returned," interposed the angel. "The lad hath returned. He was the monk who laid the letter on thy chair."

For a long time all was silent in the long avenue chequered with moonlight.

"Belisar is dead," at length said the angel.

"Then he is dead," slowly responded Justinian; and the words seemed but an echo, without regret or care or admiration or resentment.

"Heart of the nether millstone!" sighed the angel, "how greatness hath made thee little, and magnificence mean, and loyalty thankless, and truth unbelieving. What demon of pride and vainglory is it that possesses thee? How shall I move thee?"

Again there was a long silence.

"Look!" said the angel, "I will show thee the things that are to come."

Then Justinian beheld a great city given over to pillage, and he knew it was Constantinople. For three days of carnage and plunder and sacrilege a licentious soldiery raged through the blood-drenched and burning streets. The splendid monuments of ancient days which made the city the wonder of the world were carried off or shattered to fragments. Horses and mules, laden with wrought silver, jewelled crosses and chalices, and the treasures of altars and shrines, stumbled over the defiled pavement of the churches. In Sancta Sophia "a daughter of Belial" was enthroned on the seat of the Patriarch, and drunken revellers danced round with blasphemous songs.

"These warriors of the red cross," said the angel, "are vowed to rescue the sepulchre of the Lord from the heathen. They have turned aside from their sacred enterprise to ravage a Christian city and to establish a new realm. Look again!"

In one of the violated churches they beheld a magnificent sarcophagus broken open. It contained a sovereign of bygone time— embalmed, crowned, clothed in imperial purple. The body was dragged forth and held erect amid peals of ribald laughter, and Justinian recognised that it was himself. The crown was snatched from the hoary head; the jewels plucked from neck and arms. The rich robes were rent away. Naked as he was born into the world, the emperor was flung aside for the dogs.

"So fleets away the glory of Justinian," said the angel.

The tumultuous streets, the smouldering palaces, the sacrilegious host of the Crusaders vanished like mist.

"Now behold the destiny of thy basilica!"

"I will not look! I will not look!" sobbed Justinian, covering his eyes with his hands. "I have sinned; I have sinned; but that I built with pure heart and clean hands, if anything be pure and clean in Thy sight. Thou knowest that I did not glory till the work was done!"

"He hath forgotten me, remembering God," thought the angel, and melted silently into the moonlight.

THE GUARDIANS OF ROME

"THUS," said the Abbot Finnian, "having kissed the hallowed earth of our Lord's country for the last time, we repaired to Joppa, and took ship for Rome. Now I come to the strangest part of my story. Many have visited the Holy Places, and many will visit them in days to come; but what I saw in Rome, that sacred city of the martyrs, eyes never looked on before; and never, I think, will the like be seen again."

The abbot sat on the steps of the cross upon the green knoll. The brethren, grouped about him on the grass, drew still closer to listen. The red and yellow leaves fluttered softly down on the little beehive huts of stone in the clearing. On the blue lough lay the warm light of the autumn sun, drowsing towards eventide.

"How we fared on the windy sea-ways," said the abbot, "there is little need to tell. At Syracuse, where doubtless we landed on the very stones trodden by Paul the Blessed, we learned that Rome was sore beleaguered. Under their young King Baduila—Totila, the Latins called him—the fair-haired giants of the Gothic forests had swept all before them, while the imperial commanders, divided by their jealousies and corrupted by luxury, pillaged the land they could not defend and revelled in shameful safety behind their fortress walls.

"The Goths encompassed the city as with a ring of iron; and at the mouth of the Tiber the one man who could yet save Italy, and that was the great Belisarius, awaited the corn-ships from Syracuse, for Rome was starving.

"The river Tiber, you must know, runs to sea in two channels, and there are two havens. Portus was held by Belisarius with a few thousand Thracian recruits, paid out of his own purse—so grudging was the emperor and so envious of his most famous soldier; Ostia was held by the Goths; between them lay the Sacred Isle, a green spot full of roses; but four miles inland from the sea Baduila had blocked the Tiber with a boom and iron chain, guarded by a bridge with a tower at each end.

"When by good providence we got safe to Portus, the place was in a hum and stir of preparation. The corn-ships had come in; Rome was to be relieved. Swift dromons, manned with archers, were loading with provisions; stout barges and fire-ships were making ready for the bursting of the boom. Despite the pressure of his affairs, the illustrious Belisarius received us. Such a man! bronzed and dark, great-statured and powerful, still in the prime of life; but, first and last, it was the proud head and the kingly eyes lit with the splendour of victory which made him master of men.

"At daybreak on the morrow the flotilla set out for the succour of Rome, and horse and foot advanced along the river-bank to support the attack. Isaac the Armenian was left in command of the station, and his one charge was to remain at his post whatever befell. Towards noon we saw clouds of smoke rising far away on the plain, and a great cheer went up for there was little doubt that the Gothic towers were burning. Perchance the boom had been broken and the dromons were rowing hard for Rome.

"Then was the daring venture brought to nought by the folly of one man. Carried away by vainglory the Armenian abandoned his trust, dashed across the Sacred Isle, and attacked Ostia with a hundred horsemen. The Goths pretended flight; the horsemen fell to plunder, and were cut down or captured by the enemy. Meanwhile clouds of arrows from the dromons swept the Gothic bridge; the iron chain was severed; the towers were set on fire, and the boom was being hewn with axes when a messenger brought Belisarius news that Isaac was a prisoner.

"The great soldier stood aghast. Then Portus, his camp, his stores, his treasure must have been captured. All was lost and his ruin irretrievable, unless he could recover them from the enemy. In an instant the retreat was sounded, and horse and foot, dromons and archers were streaming back in fiery haste to the sea-shore. He found all safe, but the victory which might have saved the Immortal City had been snatched from his hand. That night Belisarius sickened with fever, and for many days he lay between life and death.

"No worse enemy had the Romans than their own governor, Bessas, who crammed his coffers with the treasure wrung from their miseries. Bran was sold at the price of corn. The cost of wheat beggared all but the wealthiest. Dogs, mice, and nameless vermin were killed and eaten. Nettles became the common food of rich and poor. Men's faces grew green with famine. Among the rubbish heaps of the ruined palaces the patrician sank down and died clutching a handful of the stinging weeds. One poor wretch, distracted by the wail of his children for bread, led them to a bridge over the Tiber. 'Here,' he said, 'are the fields in which sorrow and hunger are unknown,' and covering his head with his robe, plunged into the yellow waters.

"At length a bribe secured what prayers had failed to obtain. The people were allowed to quit the city. Many were slain by the outposts, more perished in the open country; but a small number reached safety, and lived to look back on those evil days. Then the grasping governor brought about his own undoing. The troops were stinted of their rations. One of the gates was sold to the enemy. At dead of night twenty thousand Goths poured into the city. Rome awoke in uproar and a tumult of hurrying torches. The garrison abandoned their posts. Bessas and his creatures fled, leaving his blood-stained hoard for the spoiler.

"The Gothic ranks stood steady through the hours of darkness. With the grey of dawn the sack of Rome began; but the king had sternly marked its limits. Outrage and bloodshed were forbidden; the churches were declared sanctuaries which it was death to violate. Again and again Baduila had warned them of the retribution that follows the abuse of victory. 'Remember,' he said, 'how when we were an exulting host, two hundred thousand strong, rich in treasure, in war-gear, in horses, a little band of Greeks overthrew us. Now we are but the remnant of a people, and Italy is ours. What but this has made the difference? Of old we forgot justice, our hands were filled with violence and wickedness, and the wrath of God was laid upon us. To-day we are of one mind to be upright and just to all men, and God has been gracious. Of one thing be sure—the heavenly light forsakes a nation when it departs from righteousness.'

"Think now of the swarms of fair-haired Goths hurrying through street and square, and raiding with fierce joy and with wonder the splendid palaces of the lords of Rome. Think, too, of the despairing crowds who had sought refuge in the churches, and expected to hear the savage war-cries of the barbarians. Pope Vigilius was in exile, but the flock of Christ was not without a shepherd. The faithful Deacon Pelagius pleaded with the king to succour his starving people, and Baduila himself came with food and fed the sufferers from the altars of the saints.

"On the morrow the king announced the fate of the city to the fallen senators: 'Your wives, your children are free; you I hold as hostages. I grant your citizens their lives; but let them seek other homes. Here they can remain no longer. Never again shall this proud and ungrateful city be the stronghold of an enemy. Rome shall perish. Its walls shall be cast down. Never again shall the blood of the Goths be shed like water before them. The flames shall consume the stately buildings of which you made your boast. Your seven hills shall be a pasture, and the shepherd-lad shall pipe on the wreck of the Golden Milestone.'

"In all that glorious capital once so thronged with people scarce five hundred citizens survived. A lamentable sight it was to behold beautiful women, noble children, proud old patricians going forth with a multitude of slaves in that dishonoured exodus.

"Then began the work of destruction. The massive gates were carried off and burnt; the lofty towers were tumbled down; already a third of the giant walls had been laid in ruins when Belisarius, from his sick bed, appealed to the king to withhold his hand from that wonder of the world, which had been the growth of many centuries, of a storied line of kings and emperors. 'Pause in thy hour of triumph,' he wrote, 'and consider whether in the imperishable record of generations thou wouldst have men read, He who destroyed—or he who preserved—the world's greatest city was Baduila the Goth.'

"The plea of the great soldier, the magnificence of Rome, the heroic legend of the past, the new saga in which he himself should appear in undying splendour moved the conqueror to magnanimity. 'Tell Belisarius,' he said to the ambassador, 'that I relent and forego my revenge. The monuments of Rome shall stand unharmed, but henceforth it shall be a city of the dead.'

"Then, in a little while, the Gothic legions departed. A detachment encamped on the Alban Hills to watch Portus, and Baduila, carrying off the hostages with him, marched into the south-east. In Rome no living soul, man or beast, was left behind.

"As the days went by, the thought of this city of the dead lay upon me like a spell. I pondered over what I had been told of the talk of holy men on Mount Cassin. For as they spoke together of the Goths, the priest Sabine said, 'This king will so destroy Rome that no longer shall any man dwell therein;' but the abbot Benedict answered him, 'Not in that wise shall this city be removed, but wasted by storms and lightning and earthquake, it shall weather away within its borders.' Lo now! it seemed as if both of these foretellings were to come to pass; and I said within myself, To Rome shall I go whatever befall, so that in time to come it may be written, 'In those days of desolation pilgrims from Erin came to worship at the tombs of the Fisherman and Tent-maker.'

"How shall I tell of the amazement and the deep awe with which we entered Rome? For the first time in thirteen hundred years that spot of earth was empty and silent. The sadness and stillness of the grave had fallen upon the glory of the Seven Hills. I thought of the word of the prophet, 'Hell from beneath is moved for thee;' but there was no movement. The noise and glitter of the quellers of the world had vanished, even as summer clouds. Like the dead of old and the kings of forgotten nations, this mighty race had departed. We three alone—for I had taken Aidan and Gall with me—were living men in the desert of houses. We went together speaking under our breath, for a fear over-shadowed us as of the presence of unseen people.

"Already the wild creatures had stolen in from the Campagna, and as we looked over those wide spaces still coloured with the gold and crimson of the withering of tall fennel and thistles, we wondered how long it would be before these streets and palaces of marble would sink down in grass-grown mounds and be lost in the open wilds. On the Garden Hill the crows had swarmed back to the gigantic walnut tree which had sprung out of Nero's tomb. During the famine they had flown to the Alban Hills, rising away to the south in their winter tints of sapphire and amethyst. But stranger than these sights was the splashing of the numberless fountains, the sound of living waters in the city of silence.

"We visited the great churches. The doors were wide open. The lamps had burned out, but we found means to light them again, and that first night we slept in the sanctuary of St. Peter, singing before we lay down, 'The sparrow hath found a house and the swallow a nest, even thine altars, O Lord of Hosts.'

"Open too were the portals of the stately houses, and though at first a nameless uneasiness held us back, we entered and passed through the halls and chambers, noting wreck and ravage of such luxury and wealth as we had never dreamed of.

"The overthrow of the walls seemed the labour of giants. As we gazed on the tumbled masses, I saw in my mind's eye the trains of barbarian captives sculptured on column and triumphal arch. How had Babylon fallen; how had the radiant one been cut down, which weakened the nations! But even these gaps of destruction did not speak so eloquently of humbling and helplessness as the hollow arches from which the great gates had been carried away. The poorest hut has its hide or hurdle, but into Rome there was no one but might enter, and who should say him nay? It was as though I heard the voice of the Prophet. 'The fire shall devour thy bars, thy nobles shall dwell in the dust. Thy people is scattered upon the mountains.' And yet, had God willed, even then, in the twinkling of an eye, a breath of life might have raised a legion of kings and captains, of horsemen and chariots, so many were the statues of heroes in Rome.

"We knelt and prayed in that wondrous arena, the dust of which had been drenched with the blood of the martyrs. We walked in Nero's gardens, wherein the 'living torches ' of the tyrant burned in the darkness. We went forth beyond the Gate Capena, where, it is said, Peter fleeing from this city, met the Lord carrying His cross, and having asked, 'Lord, whither dost Thou go?' Jesus answered, 'To Rome, to be crucified again for thee.' But the sun would go down before I had finished, were I to tell of all we saw and did.

"Three days we tarried in that place of many memories, for we thought not ever to see it again. And on the third night, though I lay wearied in body, I could not sleep for the tumult and passion of soul that worked within me. I rose, leaving the others sleeping, and stole abroad. The moon was at the full, and I wandered on in its clear shining. As I approached the Forum, I was startled by the sound of flutes and cymbals, and then of voices raised in a chant such as I had not heard before. Stepping noiselessly into the deep shadows I glided into the Forum, and I saw within its moonlit space a little group of men, clothed in white, standing near an altar of incense before the Temple of Janus. The men chanted to the music of the flutes and cymbals; the incense rose in pale blue smoke; the roof and walls of the small temple, all overlaid with brass, glittered like gold in the silvery light.

Now this temple was one of the venerable relics of bygone generations, and no enemy had despoiled it. It contained the giant brazen statue of Janus of the Two Faces, whereof one was turned to the dawn and one to the setting sun. When Rome was pagan, its brazen doors were kept shut in the good times of peace and abundance, but in time of war they were thrown open for the god to march to battle with the legions.

"DO NOT SHOW YOURSELF", HE SAID, "BUT HARKEN."

"As I listened I discovered that these men were secret adherents of the old paganism, enchanters and worshippers of devils. They called upon Janus to awake, to come forth and arouse the fallen gods to resume their sway in Rome. By what evil sorcery it was I know not, but the brazen doors of the temple swung wide, and the hideous idol leaped forth with a war-cry of ancient days, which rang through the night. Far-off voices answered. The air was beaten with the rushing of many feet. The white ground was mottled with the shapes and shadows of men and women—some dark, some pallid, some shining; and then I saw it was the gods and goddesses of Rome, the fauns and satyrs, the tyrants and persecutors—shall I not rather say, demons and lost souls?—taking possession of the old-world statues of bronze and marble, and giving them a semblance of life.

"It was in my mind to fling myself into that welter of evil, when a hand was laid upon me, and in the shadow beside me I saw a man. Tall he was rather than short, old rather than young, pleasant featured yet commanding. He was bare-footed and in fisher's garb, and on his shoulder he carried an oar. 'Do not show yourself,' he said, 'but hearken! The sleepers of the Colosseum and the Catacombs have wakened. I hear their voices; I hear them coming.'

"And I too heard. The earth was stirred beneath our feet with a deep murmur; vague risings of sound came to us, as of distant harps played by the wind. Then from the Sacred Way streamed in a radiant multitude, rosy children and tender maidens, men and women in their prime, old age in its serene beauty; and as their joyous song filled the Forum,

> 'Tu Rex gloric, Christe—
> Thou art the King of Glory, O Christ.'

the spirits of the nether darkness fled before them.

"'Thou hast seen the Guardians of Rome,' said the Fisherman, and now I knew who it was that spoke to me, for until then I had not deemed that the blessed apostles walked in guise so lowly. 'Return when it is day to Portus, and say that the city hath yet many legions to defend it, and albeit the walls be fallen there is yet a host to raise them up again. Go now to thy rest for the dawn is nigh.'

"Sleep, indeed, now lay heavily upon me, so that I scarce knew when that Holy One of the Rock departed, or how I lay down again beside my companions.

"On the morrow we came quickly to Portus, and when the great captain heard that I had brought tidings, he received me without delay. I spoke as I had been bidden, and when I had told him of all I saw in Rome, he rose from his bed with new life, and forthwith all was astir again in camp and harbour.

"He himself visited the City, and on the fortieth day that it had lain desert he entered with all his troops; the Tiber was thronged with merchant ships, and the wharfs under the Hill Capitoline hummed with traffic. It was a world to see the soldiers and the peasants, who flocked in from the Campagna, stockading the trenches and roughly filling up the breaches in the walls, so that in fifteen days their vast circuit was made strong again around the Seven Hills. More helpers perchance were there with rubble and stone than any one was aware.

"Not yet had there been time to make good the great gates when Baduila returned with his Gothic swarms. They bivouacked by the yellow river and attacked at sunrise; but in the open gateways Belisarius set his best and bravest, and strewed the approaches with four-spiked caltrops—thistle-heads of iron, which put up ever one sting against a horse's hoof throw them how you will.

"Twice the assailants were beaten back, and in the thick of the fight, when the long-haired horsemen were struck down, it may be the Fisherman's oar was not far away. On the third day Baduila's standard-bearer fell. The royal ensign was snatched up from the dust with a severed hand grasping the staff.

"That was the end. The Goths drew sullenly away from the Eternal City, to whose annals they had added the strangest incident in her many-centuried story. Belisarius completed the great gates, clamped and studded with iron, and hung them in the open gateways. Even in a city protected by unseen guardians there was need for them, for the holy ones do not help us until we have done all that we may to help ourselves."

THE TWO CHARLEMAGNES

Crown of the Holy
Roman Empire

The Iron Crown
of Lombardy

WHEN King Karloman died his people offered their allegiance to his brother Charlemagne, and the two kingdoms were once more united under a single crown. But Queen Gerberga, fearing the worst for her children, fled in the depth of winter with her two little sons, and Ogier the Dane brought them safe through the Alps to the court of Desiderius, King of the Lombards.

The king took up their cause, but little good came of his championship; for when Desiderius found that nothing could induce the Pope to anoint the children with the sacred chrism as kings of the Franks, he pounced on three of the papal cities and stormed up within a day's march of Rome itself. Pope Hadrian promptly manned his walls, threatened the invaders with the curse of St. Peter, and called Charlemagne to his aid.

The vast realm of the Franks rang with the Summons to arms, and over the snowy passes the hosts of the great Karl poured down into Italy. They found the lower gorges blocked with bulwarks of stone, but the Lombards were suddenly stricken with a midnight panic and fell back in confusion on Pavia, and the armies of the north spread over the wide corn lands of Lombardy.

From the top of one of the lofty towers Desiderius and Ogier looked out over the far-off fields when they were made aware that Charlemagne was advancing. The siege and baggage trains first emerged from the low haze of dust, and when Desiderius saw how all the ways were cumbered with waggons and engines of war, "Is not Karl with this great host?" he asked. "No," replied Ogier, who had been a hostage at Charles's court.

Then appeared the troops raised in all parts of the empire— spearmen and archers, men armed with flails, with scythes, with clubs of gnarled oak; and Desiderius exclaimed, "Surely the king is with this great multitude." "No, not yet," said Ogier. "What shall we do," cried Desiderius, growing troubled, "if he can bring more than these against us?" "You will soon see what manner of king this man is," replied Ogier; "but what will happen to us I cannot tell."

Then came the mighty Paladins, whose prowess was never at rest, and the Lombard cried out in repidation, "At last this must be Karl!" but again Osier replied, "Not yet; no, not yet!"

In the rear of these battalions rode in proud array the bishops, the priests of the chapel royal, the counts of the realm; and at the sight of them Desiderius loathed the light of the sun, and fell to sobbing and stammering, "Let us go down and hide ourselves in the depths of the earth." But once more Ogier answered, "Karl is not among these. When you shall see all the fields of the harvest tossing, and the ranks of corn bending in wild gusts, and when you shall hear your rivers roaring in a deluge of iron and your bridges creaking, and the clash of arms sounding in your ears, then you may say that Charlemagne is nigh."

Scarcely had Ogier spoken when a stretch of sombre cloud rolled up in the north-west. The day grew dark; and more awful than the darkness, glimmering swords flashed out from the smoke of the cloud. Then appeared a figure of iron. It was Charlemagne.

Iron was his helm; iron sheathed his breast and broad shoulders; his gauntlets were iron; his feet were shod in iron. Of the colour and of the might of iron was the horse on which he rode. The host that rode before him, behind him, on either hand of him, were iron hearts, clad in the terror of iron. The land in all its ways and in all its fields was thronged with iron and with points of iron flashing dreadful lights.

"Behold at last," said Ogier, "the man you have so long looked to see," and sank down at the king's side in a dead swoon.

Pavia surrendered; Desiderius was dethroned; the baby princes went unharmed, but the dominion of the Lombards was ended. And "iron" was the last word in the story of this grim pageant of iron, for when Charlemagne crowned himself Lord of Lombardy, it was with the Iron Crown, which enshrined in gold and jewels one of the nails of the Crucifixion.

This was the Charlemagne of the wars of giants and the mighty conquests. There was another; a big gladsome man, with more turns and likings than a harp has strings, and as full of music. For he delighted in learning, in hunting the aurochs, in following the cross barefoot on the solemn Rogation days, in having all his merry girls about him and giving the least little maid on his knee bite and sip from his plain cup and trencher.

Seven feet he stood, in cross-gartered hose and high-laced boots— Frank fashion. His flaxen hair fell on his broad shoulders, and his soul looked out from a cheerful face and swift lively eyes. He went in homely tunic of linen or wool, bordered with coloured silk, and perchance a coat of otter-skin in winter; and over all he wore a white or a sapphire cloak, the corners of which hung low back and front, but scarce reached the knees on either side. "Warm to wear, and little to spoil," he said, laughing, to his courtiers, whom he once took to the chase in all their Eastern finery and brought back drenched and tattered; "but oh, you spendthrifts in Tyrian purple and dormouse fur and Phœnician feathers and fringes of cedar bark, how many pounds of silver have you left on the thorns and brambles?"

Yet if he was simple and sparing in his person, he opened a kingly hand when splendour was seemly. One priceless thing he ever carried in his belt and that was Joyeuse, the Sword Jewellous, which contained in a hilt of gold and gems the head of the lance that pierced our Saviour's side. And thereto he wore a pilgrim's pouch—"against my faring to Jerusalem, or, if that may not be, to remind me that our life is but a pilgrim's way, and our joy but a pilgrim's rest, and our hope a palm."

In the palace too were massive tables of engraved silver. One, which was square, displayed the City of Constantinople on the blue waters that wash at once the East and the West; one, which was round, showed the glory of Rome on the Seven Hills; but the costliest and most beautifully wrought was a similitude of the world. Here were Adam and Eve, and the Serpent on a withered tree. A narrow pass separated Mount Carmel from Sinai; and hard by the Mountains of Antioch stood the mountains of Araby, and one saw the mysteries of the earth from the Head of Europe to the deserts of the Antipodes. "And where is Frankland?" asked little Hildruda. "This is Frankland near the two great waters." "Oh, the dear silver place! cried Hildruda. "Now you tell me," said Charlemagne, "who these are," pointing to four figures outside the ring of the regions of men. "They are blowing horns," replied Hildruda; "are they wild hunters, since they have no clothes? And these two are head over heels; maybe the aurochs has tossed them!" "Nay," laughed Charlemagne, "these are the four winds that blow over the world."

Charles made them into twelve afterwards, and called them by Frankland names; and the twelve months he changed from their heathen calling to Winter-month and Mud-month, Spring-month and Easter-month, and the month of the storks and new leaves and springing flowers he named Love-month; and so with the rest, for he liked best all that was Frank and homely.

The old folk-songs and the stories of ancient kings and heroes he had collected and written down. "These," he said, "are the joy and glory of a people; never should they be forgotten; "and often he would sing those songs to the harp. So too with old customs; when they were good and kindly he would have them still observed, like that of the wayfarer, who might pluck three apples or three bunches of grapes or take three radishes, and no man would begrudge him. But if the customs might be bettered, he would change them; and thus instead of the old idols, people carried round the fields the cross with the fair image of Christ, not naked and in anguish, as we have it, but gold-crowned and clad in bright raiment; and instead of going round the budding corn with loud cries, they went singing litanies and hymns. "A pleasant and wholesome thought," he said, "that men and women should be singing away toil and care," and he would have herd and shepherd lad sing cheerily as they went afield and returned to fold and byre with their good beasts.

Nor would he abate old uses even when they touched his own greatness. Riding abroad with his train one day, he saw seated by the roadside a man, who neither rose nor uncovered, but only raised his hand to his hat. An officer of the palace went angrily towards the man. "Who art thou," he asked, "to make so small account of King Karl?" "Who art thou to ask?" said the man.

Then Charlemagne drew near, and the man arose, with a smile on his ruddy brown face. "Thou dost not know me, Lord King," he said, "but it may be thou hast heard of the Barons of the Sun, old free-holders of this land when it was yet but a clearing here and there in forest and swamp. This man who speaks to thee is one of the last of their line. They held not from town, or prince, or emperor. Neither does he. They owed no man vassalage, they rose at no man's coming, they bared their heads to no man. Neither does he. Little is left of the old fiefs, but the Barons of the Sun were ever free men." Charlemagne smiled. "Wilt thou tell me where thou livest?" "Yonder by the fir-wood," said the man. "Wouldst thou give me welcome should I come to see thee?" asked the king. "My poor house were thine, and thrice welcome shouldst thou be." "Be sure then I will come, for I am fain to talk with thee;" and Charlemagne, leaning from his horse, stretched out a hand which this chief of the old heaths and woods grasped with a proud smile.

Frank speech he called the salt of freedom, and the fearless truth-teller a third eye. It chanced at one of his feasts a captive Saxon prince was one of the guests, and when the Saxon saw how Charles and his paladins and prelates sat at table and were served on broidered cloths, while the poor sat on the bare ground, and the dogs with them, he rose from his place and spoke low in the king's ear. "Did not your Christ say that the poor were His body and in them He was received? How can you bow your head before Him whom you treat with such scorn and give but a dog's honour?" The paladins wondered to see Charlemagne blush, but he answered, "Your words are just. I have thought too little of this. But it shall be amended."

These high feasts were little to his liking, and save when majesty and honour required his presence, the great earls held them in his name, and Charles fared frugally apart, listening the while to some brave book telling of bygone days. Most of all he took pleasure in St. Augustine's goodly tome, *Touching the City of God.* "I would," he said, "I had but twelve clerks as learned and as wise as Jerome and Augustine." Whereat Alcuin, the bluff ruddy Englishman who had been the scholar of Bede's scholars, laughed outright: "Commend me the moderation of great kings. The Creator of heaven and earth had no equals to these two, and you would have a dozen!"

And work enough he could have found for a dozen; for most of his princes of the Church were worldly and unlettered beyond belief. He had released them from service in arms, but still they flaunted in silk and purple—lords of luxury and turbulence; mighty men with hawks by the river-side and hounds in the forest; burly revellers in their great tapestried halls, drinking deep, with garlanded heads, amid a tumult of music. Alcuin gave him untiring service in founding schools all over the land, and rearing a nobler generation; and now and again, as the old warrior-priests were lapped in purple and lead, Charlemagne, by good guidance, laid his hand on some worthier man.

It was scarcely by chance alone that as he hunted deep in the forest darkness closed in, and he came benighted to a little church and priest's house. The priest Amalarius gave him friendly welcome, and set such cheer as he could before him. Talking gaily and praising the sweet brown bread and the toothsome apples and the noble cheese,

Charlemagne glanced in his talk at the rich tables of abbots and prelates, whom it would better become to think of barley loaves and fishes.

STRETCHED OUT A HAND WHICH THIS CHIEF OF THE OLD
HEATHS AND WOODS GRASPED WITH A PROUD SMILE.

The simple priest shook his head and answered gently: "If we judge at all, fair lord, let it be with charity. Are not these things God's creatures for our comfort and strength in the day? One man may offend on green herbs, and another be blameless on the stalled ox. Esau was rebuked not for flesh, but for pottage; Adam condemned not for flesh but for fruit; Jonathan judged not for flesh but for honey. Elias ate flesh yet sinned not, and Abraham laid flesh before angels. And so with drink. Surely Paul's little cup of wine were less to be reproved than greed and water."

Charlemagne was well pleased, and thinking to test Amalarius yet further, he spoke slightly of the royal house. The priest's face grew troubled, and he replied: "Doubtless you say this in jest, or it may be with little thought. Yet he was a wise man who wrote, 'Revile not the king, no, not even in thought, for a bird of the air shall carry the matter.' But even if it chanced that fault might be found in the king's household, think how St. Augustine answered in such a case: 'I would not boast that my house is better than the Ark, wherein of eight men one was reprobate; or than the Lord's, in which Judas was one of the Twelve; or than heaven itself, from which the angels fell.'"

Then Charlemagne smiled and said, "Forgive me, good father; I spoke with a fool's tongue, and you have done well to chide me."

"Nay, son, not to chide, but to remind you," said the priest.

At daybreak when the king rose and would have taken to horse, Amalarius came to him and said: "You thought not that even now I go to say Mass, and that you could tarry to thank God for sleep, and safety in the night, and a glad awakening in the world."

"Nay, gladly will I stay," said Charlemagne, reddening in the grey light.

When Mass was said and the two came forth, Charlemagne took a piece of gold from his pilgrim's pouch and offered it to his host. "Great thanks," replied the priest, "I have no need for it; but if in your sport to-day you bring down a hind, very thankful shall I be to have the skin, for my poor boots are as weathered and worn as the shoes of poor pilgrims."

"So much you shall have, and more," replied Charlemagne, "were it but for that saying of St. Augustine about his house."

Home to Aix rode Charlemagne, right well pleased to have found such a priest; and not long afterwards, when the Archbishop of Treves died, he raised this single-hearted Amalarius to his high place.

As streams are green, winding in the evening sun, and blue in the cold of the morning, and yet ever lightsome to see, so the colour of the king's moods and conditions changed, but still the man remained large and lovable. He travelled far, but his fame outstripped his horses. The Moorish minstrels sang of him in Fez, and he was the joy of the story-tellers of Baghdad. Foreign princes ransacked land and sea to honour him.

Of all the kingly men who loved him, the Caliph Haroun al-Raschid was the most lavish in his gifts. He sent him perfumes and spices, coloured hangings and mantles of silk, a mirror set in gold and enamel, and a bronze clock which was a miracle of cunning. For it had crystal windows that opened, some for the day and some for the night; it showed the time, which fleets like clear wind and none can hold it, and it dropped little brazen balls on a cymbal to count the hour. At noon twelve windows opened, and twelve Persian heroes rode out in bright mail, and closed the twelve other windows which had been open since midnight.

As if that were a trivial thing, Haroun sent him Abul-abaz, which is to say the Father of Stern Brows. Isaac the Jew brought Abul-abaz. From Africa they came to Genoa, sailing in a great carrack or sea-waggon; the winter stayed them at Vercelli, because of the deep snows in the Alps; but at last, on a July evening, the Father of Stern Brows stood towering in the sun before the palace gates, with the mahout on his neck, and Isaac beside his huge pillared shoulders, and a crowd of the good folk of Aix chattering in open-mouthed wonder.

When the children got to know the friendly mind and gentleness of Abul-abaz, they delighted to make him their playmate, adorning him with garlands and ribbons, and screaming with glee as he lumbered beneath them like a hillside in motion. Charlemagne, who could crumple horse-shoes, discovered that a strong man was but a babe in the fold of the great creature's trunk. "No sage," he said to Alcuin, "could possibly be a tenth part as wise as the Father of Stern Brows looks. The lore of ages is stored in that huge prophet's head of his. His people have been Barons of the Sun from the morning of the sixth day—a more ancient race than ours. Herein you see the lofty soul of the caliph, to send so noble an ambassador between brother kings."

But of all Haroun's gifts Charlemagne prized most the keys of the Holy Sepulchre. These he sent to be in the keeping of the Bishop of Jerusalem, "for I know not," he wrote, "how long it might be before I could bring them and worship on that most sacred spot."

When Charlemagne had finished the stately chapel from which Aix-la-Chapelle took half its name, he planned to enlarge the palace. On the ground that was needed for this work a poor woman had a little hut, which she would not sell even at ten times the price given for the houses of her neighbours. "Here I was born," she said, "and here my mother died, and here my father was born, and his father before him. This is my dear home; what gold or silver can buy me another which shall be the same?"

As the officers of the palace could not persuade her, they began to threaten her with Charlemagne's displeasure. "I wonder," she said sharply, "to hear the king's servants so belie the king. You would not dare to say these things if he could hear you." "And I too wonder," said Charlemagne, when he was told of the matter, "that knowing me for what I am, you should act thus, thinking to please me." Whereupon he went himself to the woman, and bade her be neither fearful nor troubled.

"I had no fear," she answered, "for I knew the king's justice would not suffer me to be harmed. But troubled I was, because of many memories. Yet lying awake in the night I have since thought how foolish we are to cling too closely to what is ours for only a little time, even were we to live long. And moreover, at any moment wind from the heavens, or fire, or weight of snow might snatch from us what we hold too dearly. So I pray the king to take the poor house, if I may only have some otherwhere to live."

"You shall not want," said Charlemagne. But he ordered that the hut should remain untouched, as a token of how men should value justice. "To be generous," he said, "is in our own nature, but to be just we need God to give us something of His." So amid arcades of bright stone and marble columns from Rome and Ravenna stood the poor hut thatched with brown reeds. And there it remained until, long afterwards, the Northmen invaded Aix-la-Chapelle, and destroyed the palace, and stabled their horses in the noble chapel; but they could not find the spot where Charlemagne sat crowned on his throne of gold, with Joyeuse in his belt and a copy of the Gospels lying open on his knees.

GOD'S GLEEMAN

IN the days when Venerable Bede was a monk at Jarrow, there was nowhere else in England such a realm of song as the North Countrie. It was "like land, like people;" for moor and forest and fertile vale were at one time grim in wintry dourness, at another winsome in wild summer beauty. Life was hard, the age rude and turbulent; but over the length and breadth of Northumbria might be heard at fall of night the voice of the singer; and the music of bagpipe and reed-flute and harp was as familiar in fishing cotes and upland thorps as in the manors of ealdormen.

There was one wayfarer who was ever welcome whithersoever he went, and that was the Gleeman; and of all the gleemen in the North Countrie Kynewulf was in his day the foremost. Young and handsome, gay and gallant, he was widely a favourite among the great nobles, for he was of their own etheling blood, and the hand which woke the magic of the harp-strings was as deft with the sea-rovers' helm and as deadly with the sword in fight.

More than one powerful chief had tried to retain him as the singer of his house, but in vain. All the world was too full of wonder and freshness for him to rest long in any place. His heart was hot within him for joy and adventure, and in the jocund recklessness of youth he roamed from burg to burg and from manor to manor, suiting his songs to his hearers and "winning renown and glittering gold." One night he might make mirth for the peasant folk of some hedge-girt village; the next he might be a guest at one of those worldly convents in which the abbess was still a great lady, and the nuns, with their hair curled and crinkled about their brows, went in violet linen and crimson tunics with fur-trimmed sleeves and white veils fastened with rosettes of bright ribbon.

At intervals he felt the vague longing for more than even the kindly companionship of men and women can give, and the spirit of dreams led him into lonely places, where he watched with keen eyes and pure delight the wild creatures of heath and wood and sea-shore. To many of these he gave a second life in song, as gladsome to-day as it was over eleven hundred years ago; ay, and there still play in his verse some which have long vanished from the land, like the beaver of the nut-brown streams and the wild swan whose humming feathers—

> "Sounded along,
> A shining song,
> High o'er the flood and fell."

There was one pleasant spot among the hills on the northern side of the Great Wall where he had long been received like a truant son of the house who had come home again; and if folk seldom spoke there of his fame as a gleeman he was all the better pleased on that account. In this old manor of Flanging Shaw—the green wood clinging to the hillside—he had watched the thegn's little daughter Mildryth grow up from her prattling childhood. At each return from his wanderings it was still, "Why, elfkin, how you have sprung; and flowered too!" and at each departure there was the same laughing farewell, "Kiss me ere you go, and I will kiss you when you come back!" so that as time went on apace the blithe elf became to him more and more a companion when he was with her, and a sweet little soul to call to remembrance when he was far away.

It was for her that he made many of his riddle-songs, and they were called riddles because in each there was a picture of something and she had to guess what it was; and Kynewulf had a delightful way of putting all manner of pretty everyday things into these songs. There were the five sisters who lived all through the summer out in the sunshine and the rain; but when the cold weather came they had a warm house in which there was a large room and a little closet, and four of them played in the room, but the fifth, who was very masterful and often went against the others, had the closet to herself. And all of them wore little half-moons on their foreheads, and if they did not keep their moons white and clear the winter-elves tried to nip them with frost for their naughtiness. Mildryth hugged herself with glee when she found that this was a riddle-song of her fingers and her winter-mittens.

There were riddles of beasts and birds which pleased her much. The white-muzzled brock, or badger, sang to her out of his burrow, telling her how he ran through the grass on his sharp pointed toes, and how, when his enemies came digging at the entrance of his earth, he had to tunnel a street through the hillside for his dear little folk to win their way out to safety. Once too when Mildryth looked up at the branching antlers of the stag at the end of the roof-beam, Kynewulf made the great creature speak to her of his swift springing flights to the sunny hilltops, of his raids on the green meadows, and of the hard winters when he shook the hoar-frost from his head and dug down through the frozen snow for food. How often, too, had the old forest trees shrouded him and his comrade on stormy nights! Then his voice rose, belling in sorrow —

> "High on the roof-beam all alone I bide;
> No brother here in winter or summer tide!
> Where art thou, fleet-hoof, who wast wont to range
> O'er dewy turf with me, and crackling snow?
> Where gleams thy branchy head, I do not know,
> Whether on purple moor or gabled grange."

"Oh, poor stag!" cried Mildryth. "Let me repeat it thrice, and I shall have it without book."

Then there was the riddle of the swifts on a summer evening —

"Airily up-floated,
Here are little wights,
Rushing, dusky-coated,
Flecked with sunny lights;
Winding high in esses,
Hawking down again
Round the wildwood nesses,
Round the roofs of men;
Racing, shrilling, jinking
In a madcap game,
While the sun is sinking.
Hear them shrill their name!"

These things had begun in the early days when Kynewulf used to remind her at table that "little wights took little bites; "but now the tricksy elf had grown into the little Lady Mildryth; and in these last months of the gleeman's wandering life it happened more than once that after he had turned his horse's head towards Hanging Shaw and galloped forward a mile or two, he suddenly drew rein and took another track. But call her what they might, the little Lady Mildryth was still very much the same sprightly elfkin; and that Kynewulf would have guessed, if he had seen her gazing eagerly across the meadows and wondering what it was that kept her merry friend so long away.

Now it chanced in the autumn that Kynewulf was present at a high feast in one of the gay houses where a jovial warrior was lay abbot, and during the merry-making that night it seemed to him three times as though some one had plucked his sleeve, and he was somehow aware that the elfkin stood invisibly beside him. A strange lightness of heart came over him, so that folk wondered at the wild spirit of mirth which laughed in his eyes and rang out in his voice. He rose early in the same happy mood and rode away northward, thinking to himself, "To-night I sleep in Hanging Shaw even if I borrow an hour of the starlight. I have been too long away, and with a fool's reason."

Companions fared with him some distance on the way, then parted east and west, while he went on alone, humming snatches of song and taking pure joy in the colour of the world. There was a mist on the far hillsides; dew sparkled on the gossamer; in a meadow shone a birch-tree, a silvery trunk with a cloud of orange gold against the blue sky. In a high rounded field churls were ploughing, and the teams of oxen went over the swell of the land like great ships sailing slowly; and one side of the furrow was black, and one was green with the growth of heart's ease in the stubble, which the ploughshare had not yet turned over and buried.

In the afternoon the road ran through tracts of heather. Near the wayside a shepherd lad sat piping on a grey moor-stone, and a cross of green rushes lay upon the stone, and beside the cross were scrawled in chalk three runic letters— F, B, and P.

"Hail, aged sire!" cried Kynewulf as he approached him, "How many sheep hast thou to thy charge?"

"Two score and five, lord." answered the lad.

"Dost thou know every one of them?"

"Ay, lord; and they know me, and my pipe and my horn."

"That is as it should be with true shepherds. I see thou hast the cross with thee."

"Ay, lord; for here be moor-pools, haunted by water-elves."

"And what signs are these thou hast written in chalk?"

"That, lord, methinks thou knowest," answered the lad with a smile. "These be 'Oak' and 'Birch' and 'Thorn'; and in oak and birch and thorn is strong magic against sprites and dwarfs and dwimers and fierce witch-wives."

"But these are not the things themselves, only signs of them," said Kynewulf.

"Nay, this is 'Oak' and this is 'Thorn,' and this oak and this thorn is as mighty as any that ever grew in ground. Folk do say they be even mightier than the living trees, and this oak and thorn and others of their kind have such craft that they can stay ships upon the sea, and win love and hate, and cast folk into slumber, and raise up them that are dead. I know not. Canst thou believe it, lord?"

"Ay, can I, and do," replied Kynewulf laughing, "though perchance not quite in the way thou thinkest. Here, wise man of the moor, is a fee to thee"—dropping some coins into the lad's hand. "Fair fortune and long life!"

"And better still to thee, lord!" said the shepherd lad.

It was wearing towards evensong when man and beast stayed awhile for their last rest at Hagulstad, the fair town which is now called Hexham; and when Kynewulf rode on again, the low red light of the west was beginning to dwindle in the woods which overhung the way to the Great Wall.

Grey moths fluttered out of the shadows. Bats flitted noiselessly by in freakish swervings. Trees and rocks lost their outlines in the uncertain twilight. Kynewulf was wishing that he were at large again under the open sky when a faint sound of chanting reached his ears, and a few moments later the dusky road flickered with the flames of far-off torches. "It is some procession of monks," he thought, "making their way homeward to the Abbey at Hagulstad."

As the distance lessened, the flare of the moving lights revealed a company of darkly-hooded figures, and in the mournful chant he recognised the supplication of the Penitential Psalms; but it was not until he had reined his horse aside to let the procession pass that he perceived how in the midst of them four of the brethren carried a bier shoulder-high, and over the bier lay a white pall.

Behind the smoky blaze of the torches came a train of mourners, but so startling had been the discovery that this was a pageant of the grave, that Kynewulf scarce noticed the solitary man who rode in front of them with bowed head. After him rode other horsemen, and then the road was black with a great company on foot.

Dimly visible the crowd moved by with a strange sound of trampling in the dark, and that muffled beat of footsteps passing away was more lamentable to hear than the dirge of the hooded men.

A white pall and but four bearers! Suddenly Kynewulf became aware that some little maid had gone down the dusty way into the stillness beyond the world. He leaned from his saddle and spoke to one of the mourners.

"Tell me, good friend, who is dead?"

"The sweetest maiden under heaven, God rest her soul! It is the little Lady Mildryth of Hanging Shaw."

"No, no, man, no! That cannot be. Tell me thou art not sure."

"Ah, sure as the good thegn, who rides yonder with never a word to say."

"O God in the high heavens! When did this happen?"

"This is the fourth day; she was ailing but a little while; we bear her to her rest in the abbey."

"I thank thee. There is no more to say. Go, man, go!"

Cold and motionless as stone, Kynewulf sat gazing, long after the torch-light had flickered away; but still he saw the bier and the white pall, faring onward and onward into the darkness but never disappearing, and still he heard the trampling of feet, the muffled sound of generations passing for ever from fire and the light of the sun and the homes of men.

NO, NO, MAN, NO! THAT CANNOT BE—TELL ME THOU ART
NOT SURE.

And Mildryth was dead—dead! Never more would her bright face be turned up to him; never more would he hear her merry laughter. With the wailing "Ea-la! Ea-la!" of a woman, he plunged through the darkness, heedless what became of him or whither he went. The little elf of sweetness and joy! lost, blown out like a light in the wind; ea-la!

Out upon the cold waste beyond the Wall a deep gloom fell upon his mind, and the sins and follies of his reckless life crowded into memory. He felt himself outcast and accursed. The very runes of his name changed into living things and fluttered duskily round him in care and anguish. "K and Y and N are we, and into what trouble hast thou brought us!" Then he was seized with an unspeakable horror of he knew not what, and a shrieking fear made him leap from his saddle and cling screaming to his dumb companion. The horse rubbed its head against him, and when the wild fit passed he walked for a long way beside it with his hand twisted in its mane.

For many days reason and memory failed him. Whither he wandered, how he found food, where he slept, by what good guidance he escaped the perils of the waste he never knew. When at length the cloud lifted from his brain, he was standing, grey-haired and ragged, in the sunlight before a tall cross of stone. It was carved all over, here with runes and there with vine-leaves, and little creatures among them; but the man's gaze was fixed on the runes, which were the voice of the cross speaking. As Kynewulf read, it told how it had lifted on high the mighty King, the Lord of the heavens; how it was drenched with His blood; how folk came from afar to look upon Him, and it was overwhelmed with sore sorrow.

Weeping bitterly, Kynewulf fell upon his knees and laid his head on the step of the cross. While he lay there an aged priest came by, and after watching him some time he drew near and touched him.

"Rise, son; it may be that I can help thee."

Kynewulf arose, and looked at the priest with piteous eyes, but spoke no word. The priest saw that his face was noble, his hair grizzled before its time, and his garb rich despite its disarray. Putting his arm within Kynewulf's, "Tell me," he said, "how thou hast come hither, for thou art not of these parts."

"It were long to tell," replied Kynewulf, pressing his hand on his brow, "and I have forgotten many things."

"Come with me then, for thou art in need of repose," and the priest led him to a little thorp enclosed within its dyke of stakes and quick-set thorn, and so to his home in the church. He laid food before him, and when Kynewulf had eaten and drunk, he told who he was and whence he came and all that had befallen him.

"Be of good cheer, son," said the old priest, "for assuredly thy angel has been with thee. Now take thy rest, and fear no evil."

All that day from noon until sunset and far into the darkness Kynewulf lay dreamless in the heavy sleep of the sorrowful. But at the dead hour of the night, when his outworn spirit had been made new, he beheld once more the cross, in a vision. It was not now a carved stone, but a great rood of wood, wonderful, wreathed with light, and casting aloft bright beams into the heavens. All the wood of the forest was glazed over with gold; the foot of it was crusted with gems and gems were on the shoulder-span.

While he gazed upon it, he saw that this tree of glory was ever changing in its colour and clothing; now it was wet and crimson with blood, and now again dazzling with gold and jewels; and out of the vision, as it thus came and went, a wind of song told its story, from the ancient days when it was felled at the end of the weald, and reared up on a hill, and swung on high men outlawed—wolf-heads; from those ancient days unto that eventide when the Lord of Victory, lifted down from His pain, was laid in a grave of clean stone, and the poor folk sang a lay of sorrow over Him, and wending away out-wearied, left Him at rest with a little company.

Long afterwards Kynewulf wrought that dream into a noble Song of the Rood, but now, lying on the sheer brink of perdition, he was overjoyed to hear the voice calling to him: "Loved listener of mine, bid all men to this beacon; on me the Son of God hung in anguish, and they may each one be healed who with awe behold me, for I have opened the true way of refuge."

Kynewulf awoke, praying earnestly to the cross, and eager to die; but the morning brought another day and a new life.

When he had regained his strength and clothed himself anew, he bade the good priest farewell. The old man held his hand for a little while, looking with much love into his face.

"I am glad to have known thee, son, though I think not ever to see thee again. But good things abide for thee in thy east country, and not the least of them is to have the counsel and solace of my brother Beda. Do not fail to take my greeting to him."

So it fell out that Kynewulf came to Jarrow. It was in the winter, and the low green hill was drifted with snow, and Tyne Water and the great pool where the king's ships lay were covered with ice; but Father Beda was as friendly as fire in the ingle nook, and for all his fame gracious and lowly, and despite his busy life at leisure to speak with him. He heard all his confession and counselled him on the ordering of his life.

"The cowl does not make the monk, nor the tarred rope the sea-rover. Think many times ere betaking thee to the cloister. Thy gifts are of the age, and such evil as thou hast done was in the age. I would have thee remain there and be God's Gleeman. Was not blessed Aldhelm wont to stand on the bridge and in the market-place singing English songs, so that he might draw folk to him to hear the Lord's Word?"

"Ea-la!" sighed Kynewulf, "I sing no more. My gift has been taken from me."

"So it is with the birds when the old feathers fall. Let thy new feathers be grown, white and clean, and thou wilt sing again."

"Nay, the wells are dry and all the blossom of the world is withered."

"Never think it," said Beda cheerily. "The wells and the flower of the world are in each man's heart. Now listen to me, for though it seldom happens that any one can give to another such vision of things as he himself hath, I will tell thee of matters that folk talk of, but that a gleeman might better sing of, and so save them for the years that are to come. Didst thou ever hear the legend of Thomas Didymus—how when the Lord would have him carry His Gospel unto Ind and Taprobane he was a slow-heart and loath to go; and the Lord said, 'Nay, but go thou shalt,' and casting a rope about his neck, He hailed Thomas to the haven where the Eastern ship folk trafficked, and sold him for a slave. But the chapman, somewhat in doubt; took Thomas aside, and questioned him, 'Art thou indeed this man's slave?' and Thomas answered eagerly, 'Yea, yea, truly He is my Master though I be the basest of His bondsmen.'"

The light kindled in the gleeman's eyes, but Beda raised his hand and went on: "Here is a thing, as it were but of yesterday. Thou knowest how the holy Augustine came to Canterbury. He that consecrated him was Virgilius, Bishop of Arles; and before he was bishop he was abbot in Lerins Isle. As he walked of a night round that island, like a faithful shepherd round the wattled fold, he came upon a strange ship lying close against the shore, and upon the deck he saw mariners in the starlight. Two came down the gangway and greeted him. They were bound, they said, to the Holy Places, and they had put in to the island hoping that they might win him to sail with them, for they had heard of his holiness and his austerity, and no truer pilot might they have to that sacred land. Virgilius smiled grimly as he heard their praise, and he lifted up his hand and made the sign of the cross. Ship and mariners vanished, and in the dark waves he saw but the glimmering of the stars."

And Kynewulf's eyes shone like stars. "Tell me more," he cried; "the thought of these things is new to me."

"What a lay too mightest thou make," said Beda, "of the holy Guthlac in his isle among the black waters of the bright-flowering Fens! Or if thou shouldst wish for a loftier theme, hast thou not: *In exitu Israel de Egypto*? Or, now that I think of thy dream, what dost thou say to the quest of Elene the Empress who found the blessed wood on which the Lord died? Then, high over all—when thou hast won to the strength and happy peace of thy manhood—wilt thou not sing of the Lord Himself, thy Christ and mine, who came to us a naked babe, and who will come yet again in the clouds on that day when the dead shall be as glass, showing within them all the hidden things of life, and thy rood-tree of light shall take the place of the fallen stars and the darkened sun?"

"Who shall be equal to such mighty minstrelsy?" asked Kynewulf.

"That, I said, was for the day of thy strength and tranquillity," replied Beda. Then turning over the smooth vellum leaves of a Greek book, and reading a little here and there, "When Matthew was a captive among the Mermedonians," he continued, "the Lord appeared to Andrew in a dream, and bade him hasten to the deliverance of his brother. But Andrew shrank aghast from the perils of the deep and the terror of waters and the naked earls of man-eating folk. The Lord's sorrowful rebuke brought him to a stouter heart; and early in the morning he went down with his disciples to the sea-shore. There he beheld a white ship with sun-browned mariners three, and these were the Lord Himself and two of His angels in the guise of foreign ship-folk. Andrew hailed them, 'Ho! ye bold sea-roamers, whither are ye bound?' The master-shipman answered, 'To Mermedonia.' 'Thither, too, would we,' said Andrew. ''Tis a wicked coast,' said the Lord, 'and ill fare strangers landing there.' 'None the worse should we fare, if we might sail with you in this white ship with the green wales. Wilt thou take us?' 'Right willingly,' he answered, 'when ye have paid fee and charge, as we shall bargain.' 'No charge can we pay,' said Andrew, 'for we carry nor scrip nor purse; nay, nor bread nor shoes, but God will provide for thy payment.' Then laughed the shipman, sitting high on the bulwark, 'What manner of folk are ye that would wander far on the heaving street of ocean, having not imaged gold, nor yet arm-rings, nor any sort of treasure?' 'We are God's men,' said Andrew, 'wending whither He bids us.' 'Ah,' said the Lord, the mariner, 'if you be God's men, I must needs take you freely'." And looking up from the book, "Does it weary you?" asked Beda.

"No, no; say on," replied Kynewulf.

"When the white ship was far away from the pleasant land, storm-winds rose, the seas cried out to each other, and the Terror of Waters came upon them, so that the disciples were afraid. Andrew strove to comfort them: 'Take courage! It was on such an evening as this, long ago, that the great storm broke upon us from the hills, so that the waves beat into our ship, and our Master, as you know, was sleeping. Now He sleeps not nor slumbers, and leaves unhelped no man on earth whose courage does not fail him.' The storm died down, and in the stillness of the night Andrew and the Lord, the helmsman, talked together: 'In my youth I was a fisher, like Simon my brother, and through many gales have we run in our sea-boat, but never have I seen mariner like thee to steer through wet wind and sea-smoke. I would I had thy art.' 'That I might perchance teach thee,' said the Lord, the steersman; 'but what was that I heard thee say of one who slept in a great storm?' And Andrew told Him of the quelling of the winds and the stilling of the sea. 'What more dost thou remember of thy Master?' asked the Lord. 'Many a day it would take to tell thee all,' said Andrew, and as the ship bore on in the starlight he recalled the days of the Lord's companionship, until his eyes grew heavy. When he awoke it was morning, he was on the shore of Mermedonia, and he roused his companions, crying, 'Awake, arise; it was Christ who was our steersman.'"

Beda was still speaking when the bells rang for vespers, and he broke off and quickly closed the book. "Come," he said; "the angels, I know, visit the canonical hours and gatherings of the brethren. If they found me not there, would they not say, 'Where is Beda that he does not come with the brethren to the prescribed prayers?'"

Thus in the cloister on the low green hill of Jarrow Beda sought to school Kynewulf to his new life as God's Gleeman.

When Easter had gone by and birch-tree and rowan were in tender leaf, Kynewulf set out to the home of dear memories at Hanging Shaw. There he abode awhile, taking and giving such solace as he might. In the midst of May he received tidings of the death of Beda on the eve of Ascension. "Why was I not there?" he said; and thinking how that holy man lay alone in his cell, with but one scholar writing by his side, while the brethren were abroad with the cross, making the circuit of the fields and beseeching a blessing on the fruits of the earth, he marvelled at the strange endings of the lives of men.

Thereafter he fared south to Hagulstad for the feast of Pentecost. On that day of the rushing wind and the tongues of fire, as he stood by the little elf's place of rest, the Lord and Light-bearer gave him back his gift of song, made pure in the fire and free from shame.

When he returned once more to his wandering life, folk scarcely knew again the gay singer in the man who had shrieked on the waste and whose young hair was dashed with grey.

Some of the themes that Beda taught him he wrought into noble verse, and men listened to them with quickened pulses. He won to his day of strength and tranquillity, and sang the Dream of the Rood which he had seen long ago in sleep. He was then an old man, with very few friends left on the earth. They had fared hence and had their abiding in heaven.

When he too passed away from this fleeting life, I do not know. Best pleased am I to think of him as a shadowy gleeman, untouched by time, and flitting about the Northumbrian moors continually.

IN THE DAYS OF ATHELNEY

SEVEN years did the monks of Lindisfarne wander over Old Northumbria with the body of St. Cuthbert. In the wildest tracts of that wide land of fell and forest there was no spot the saint in life had ever seen to which they did not bring him in his shrine; and further still they bore him than he had ever travelled.

Evil was the day that brought about that long and strange wayfaring with the holy dead. For after Halfdene had sacked and burned the priory of Tynemouth, he and his Danish sea-wolves swept northward, harrying the unprotected coast. But swiftly as they sped, dismay and fear flew faster; and before the dragon-prows dashed into the bay at Lindisfarne, the little brotherhood, carrying in tears the shrine of their beloved saint, had escaped along the ridge of sand left bare between isle and mainland at ebb of the tide, and gathering their churls and tenants, with the flocks and herds of the abbey, had fled for refuge to the high moorland.

One brother alone, who had been bidden to stay and watch, saw the sea-wolves leap ashore in their ring-shirts and iron-winged helms, and beheld that noble abbey and its stately church pillaged and reduced to ashes.

Think now of those houseless fugitives in the bitter weather of the early spring. It is night, and you can trace but dimly the dark outlines of the wild heath, rolling away, waste beyond waste, under the icy stars. Out on the eastern knolls men keep watch to seaward. Dogs guard the sheep and cattle huddled among the gorse and broom. Down in a hollow, sheltered from view, fires are burning; and around these the poor folk—men and women, with their children and their old people—lie close for warmth. Under a leafless ash-tree rests the precious shrine, and beside it Bishop Eardulf and Eadred, the gentle Abbot of Carlisle, sleep for sorrow, when they sleep at all.

The cold wind moans; the keen stars shift over-head. The little children cry, and are hushed to sleep again. The watch is changed; the turf grows stiff and whitens with frost. Away yonder in the holy island the ruins are still smouldering, and the sea-wolves carouse on the long-ships in the bay. O Cuthbert, servant of God, how long wilt thou suffer these things and make no sign?

The saint lies in his coffin, but not as one who has been dead well-nigh two hundred years. Lifelike he lies, and comely in alb of linen and golden stole; his face ruddy, rather long; his brown hair and slight beard sprinkled with silver; his feet sandalled. Mortality and time have left him without blemish. A breath of God, and he would arise, unchanged in form and feature as though he had trod these hills but yesterday. The head of Oswald the king and relics of Aidan and Venerable Bede lie beside him in his coffin. These are crumbling into dust, but Cuthbert only slumbers. So his people think of him, resting in his shrine.

On the morrow began that long wayfaring.

And first, seven stalwart laymen were chosen to bear the coffin, and with it that great book of the Gospels which Bilfrid cased in gold and silver work inlaid with gems, and which was so fair writ and illuminated with such beauty that even to this day it is held a marvel. The names of five of these staunch comrades remain— Hunred and Stitheard, Edmund and Franco and Eilaf; and long after Cuthbert had been laid in the peace of the great church on the wooded cliffs above the Wear, their goodly service was the boast of their descendants.

But as for the rest, saving only Abbot Eadred and Eardulf the Bishop, there is no remembrance at all. They have all gone—drifted like leaves, scattered like mist; the names of husband and wife and little children and lovers, once so dear, are now clean forgotten. How many they went forth, by what roads and wild tracks they journeyed, how they were turned hither and thither in a land overrun with fire and sword no one can tell. Churches and crosses marked in later days the spots where they had rested little or long, with their hallowed burden; and these were dotted over the wide shires, from Melrose and Kirkcudbright (which is Cuthbert's Kirk) to the rocks and tarns between Coniston and Windermere, and from Ribble waters and Lytham sands to the deep woods of the squirrels of Craike.

I see them passing as in a dream. I see their faces, I hear their voices as in a dream. Their faces are brown, and worn, and rugged, but their eyes are bright with courage. Their hymns float over the springs of Tyne; the shepherd hears them on the Furness fells. They live in tents and caves; their fires burn on ancient hearths, on the broken Roman Wall; they sleep among the purple heather and in huts of green boughs. Now I lose them in the smoke of the autumn rains; now snow lies deep, and the midnight skies are aglow with the Northern Lights. To-day a little child dies; they will never again weep over its cairn on the waste. To-morrow an aged man will drop, and they will dig his grave in the trampled garth of a ruined church.

I see them on the Cumbrian shore. In England, alas! they have no more hope, they say, to live peacefully. Beyond the seas are the green hills of Erin, where the sun shines, and they dream of a fair cloister where at last their saint may rest. But the winds rise, and the white surf beats them back to land.

Over this ravaged countryside famine has fallen, and deadly sickness. The barns are empty, the fields are unplanted. The wanderers are worn out; they can go no further. And St. Cuthbert gives no help. Some lie down and die; others steal away into the hills, to live in such fashion as they may.

Even the strength of the bearers has failed. But one of them sees in the brightness of sleep such a spot as they may have passed with little notice; and thither friendly strangers beckon him. At sunrise he and his fellows come to the place. 'Tis a death-stricken farm. In the wood hard by a roan horse runs up whinnying, and nuzzles them for loneliness. In the sheds they find harness, and a light dray whereon they may place the shrine. In the deserted house a little meal has been left in the meal-kist. Thus once again they turn with better cheer into new ways.

Now it was in the third year of the wandering that Alfred the King lay in the marshes of Athelney. May-time it was, apple-bloom on the tree and the cuckoos calling; but black care sat by the hearth in the little island bulwark. Never yet had the king's fortunes fallen so low, or he been cast into such straits.

Upon a certain night, as he sat at board with his scant companionship of trusty thegns, he saw how heavy and dismayed they showed. And saying within himself, "Keep me, good Lord, on the sunny side of despair, for if I too lose heart all is lost," he cast about for some brave tale of other days to lighten their spirits.

Then, taking his little son upon his knee, "Stout kinsman," said he, "I would have you know that far away towards the rising sun lie the two halves of the world, East and West, and narrow seas race between them. Upon the eastern side Darius was in old time King of Kings and lord over many nations—Assyrians, Medes, Persians, and an innumerable people. But upon the western side Athens, a city resplendent with temples and houses of white stone, sat on a hill by the shore; a blue bay before it, and behind it the mountain Hymettus which glows at sundown with a wondrous violet light. And that, it may be, was why Athens was by-named the City of the Violet Crown.

"Now upon the eastern side were rich cities of the Greeks along the Ionian shore; and when the King of Kings would have brought these to serfdom, the men of Athens sailed on twenty ships to aid their kinsfolk, and marching inland they burned down his city of Sardis for the king, and got them back to sea with their spoil.

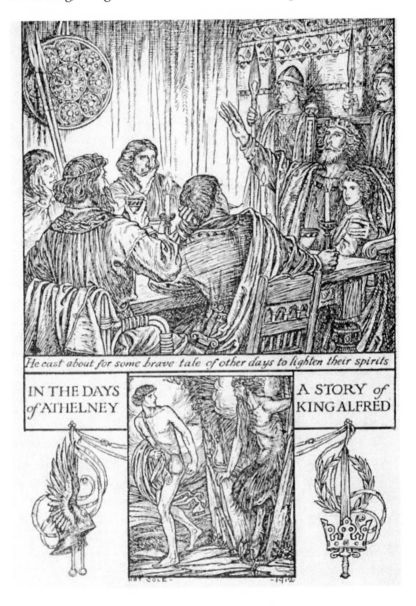

He cast about for some brave tale of other days to lighten their spirits

IN THE DAYS of ATHELNEY

A STORY of KING ALFRED

"Wild as fire in dry reeds was Darius. He called the slave who fanned him at his meat. 'While Athens stands,' he said, 'do thou repeat three times each day, Master, remember the Athenians!' To all the states of Hellas heralds were out demanding earth and water in token of submission, 'For under the wide heavens,' said the king, 'we are the lord and givers of these.' Many of the Greek cities cried craven and paid the tribute; but at Athens the herald was flung into a pit, at Sparta he was cast into a well, while the people jeered, 'Earth and water! take there as much as Darius needs!'

"And three times, day after day, the slave who waved the fan of peacock's feathers repeated his cry, until at length a mighty host was gathered, and six hundred long-ships—great triremes that whitened the seas with sounding oars—bore into the west, and every ship carried fetters and chains for the men of Hellas. The Cyclades were wasted, the island cities destroyed, and landing on Eubœa the Persians laid siege to Eretria.

"Then was Athens distracted between the wisdom of valour and the folly of dismay. But when Eretria fell the councillors of Athens sent for the swift runner Pheidippides; and when he came before the archons sitting in their marble seats, with golden grasshoppers in their hair, they saw how tall and slim he stood, deep-chested, lean as a hound, with light, sinewy limbs, sandaled shapely feet, and eager eyes that seemed to drink distance in. And they smiled for pleasure in his goodliness.

"'Thou art our fleetest,' said one of the grave men; how long to Sparta?'

"''Tis fifty leagues, and over mountains; but starting now, and Hermes helping'—for Hermes, kinsman, was one of their gods, and his shoes were winged—'surely I may catch the gleam of the Brazen House in the morning that follows to-morrow.'

"'To Sparta, then! And thus shalt thou say on coming into presence of the magistrates: "O Lacedemonians, the men of Athens entreat you to assist them, and not to suffer the most ancient city among the Greeks to fall into bondage to barbarians. Eretria is already reduced to slavery, and Hellas has become weaker by the loss of a renowned city." But do thou, young man, rejoice in thy strength, and if ever thou hast run swiftly, make now still better speed for Athens.'

"Then was it up and away for Pheidippides, a pebble closed in each hand, and the lithe body poised upon feet supple and springy as a yew bow. Through the passes of Ægaleos he sped; round the sweet-wooded bay by the sacred road to Eleusis; past Megara, and along the Evil Staircase hung on the face of the Scironic cliffs. Orchards, villages, temples, tombs, statues of gods and goddesses fleeted by; but the great mountains seemed to go with him, moving with slow might, loath to part from him, and then, as it were, passing him on, one to the next—a man to befriend for the sake of Athens.

"So running and running, resting a while to eat and drink, stopping to sleep, his steady pace carried him into the south within gladsome vision of the sea. Next, away to westward he swerved, entered the narrow defiles, climbed through the rocks and sombre pines over the mountain masses, until at last there, in the morning sun, were the snowy domes of Taygetus, there the streams of Eurotas flowing in a land of corn, and the Brazen House of Sparta, the goal of the fifty leagues, gleamed over the orange groves.

"'O Lacedemonians, the men of Athens entreat you.'

"Did the fall of Eretria bring a flush to the Spartan faces? Was the pride of Sparta stung with a thought of the conquest of Hellas? Nay, but in their scornful lips and the furtive eyes of those who heard him he read hatred of Athens, envy of her glory, and malicious joy at her danger.

"His heart was hot within him, and hotter still it burned when they gave their answer: 'Can Sparta be stone when Athens is suppliant? Tell your archons this: When the moon rises full on the mountains Sparta takes the field. Sooner it may not be, for such is our old-time observance of law. Till then we wait in patience, reverencing the gods.'

"'I have heard,' he said; 'I remember; give me leave to depart with your answer.'

"A moment he paused to tighten his belt; he waved aside the offer of food and rest; speeding fleeter than ever he reached the Eurotas, and on the bank of the river he loosened his sandals and washed the dust of Sparta from his feet. And 'O you gods,' he cried as he fell into the measured tread of the fifty-league runner, 'to you, when our own kind fail us, we come at the end.'

"Crossing the plain, he ascended the track of barren stone on the flank of Parthenon. There in the desolate gorges, where the mother-rock was rifted and scattered, he heard himself called by name. He turned, and gasped as he saw in a cleft of the mountain Pan the earth-god, in form half-man and half-goat. But the awful being looked graciously upon him and bade him draw near.

"'Why,' he asked, 'has Athens alone of the cities in Hellas no thought of me who wish her well? Not once or twice in times gone by have I been friendly to her, and so will I be again. Already I hear far off the plunging of ships and the shouting of the sailors; but bid Athens mark how, when the thin line of battle wavers and breaks in the fennel meadows, Pan will hold his place with her bravest. And thou,' said the god with a grave smile, 'thou hast run well for Athens, shalt fight well for Athens, and shalt not go without reward.'

"Before Pheidippides was aware, the earth-god vanished and was one again with soil and stone, and nothing remained but the cleft in the mountain where he had sat.

"So, while Sparta waited for the full moon, the men of Athens took their stand at the head of the only road by which the Persians could advance on the city. Here the mountains drew back in a crescent from the sea, and left the green plain of Marathon, where the fennel flowered; and at each end of the crescent deep swamps filled the space between the road and the sea. They chose their ground on the rise at the foot of the mountains, and extended their formation across the breadth of the plain. There were neither horsemen nor archers.

Their strength was massed in the wings; but their numbers scarce sufficed to fill the shallow ranks in the centre. The fate of Hellas depended that day on ten thousand men, and a gallant eight hundred sent by Platæa in grateful remembrance of help received from Athens.

"Along the shore the invaders swarmed from the great ships; and spearmen, archers, and slingers, chariots and cavalry fell into dreadful array, one hundred and ten thousand strong.

"For a moment Athens looked into the face of Asia, and then such a thing was done as men had never seen in the wars of the world. At a signal given, the whole Greek line, raising its cry of battle, swept down the rise at a run. North and south, the heavy wings shattered the Persian front, and rolled back horse and man into the marshes and the sea. But the centre wavered, broke, fled, but raffled, and as the rays of the setting sun streamed into the faces of the enemy, a rustic armed with a ploughshare stood in the broken line, and held a thousand at bay. More than a mortal man he seemed, and when the day was won he vanished, as Pan had vanished in the cleft of the mountain.

"Such was Marathon fight. Seven of the great ships burning lighted the Persian fleet to sea. More than six thousand of the enemy fell. Athens lost one hundred and ninety men.

"Once again the runner of runners plied his speed, bearing these tidings to Athens: 'Pan fought for us; Hellas is free.'

"Six-and-twenty miles, by the road the Persians never should come, Pheidippides flew, reached the glorious city at dusk, and panted out his message. Then his breath failed, his heart stopped. To die with those words on his lips—what better reward than that could life bestow?"

"What a fight was that!" "What a runner!" "What a god to help!" rang through the hall as Alfred finished his story.

"Little kinsman," said the king, "call Athelney Athens, and we too have a God who in times gone by has often been friendly to us; ay, and so will He be again!"

As the king lay awake that night thinking of many things, the place was filled with a soft shining, and a man stood near him in an alb of white linen and a golden stole. His face was ruddy and somewhat long, and his brown hair and slight beard were sprinkled with silver. Starting from his pillow, the king cried out, "Stand! who art thou?" The tall man told him his name and why he had come; and he bade him free his mind from too much care, and go forth strong-hearted, for in six days he should overcome his enemies. "And this shall be the sign. Rise up early and blow thine horn thrice, and three hundred men shall come to thee, harnessed for battle."

In the morning King Alfred rose and sailed to the land. Three times he blew his horn; and thrice he was answered, and the friend of his heart, Ethelnoth the Ealdorman, came to him through the fens with three hundred men at his back. Breathless then was the running and riding east and west. The beacon was lit on the edge of Selwood Forest, and the men of Hampshire, the men of Wiltshire, the men of Somerset flocked to Egbert's Stone.

Three days thereafter the king won the crowning battle of Ethandune. At the turning-point of the fight his standard-bearer was slain, but the standard was caught and held aloft by a tall man in a white alb and golden stole. Some said this was St. Neot, the king's kinsman, but I say St. Cuthbert.

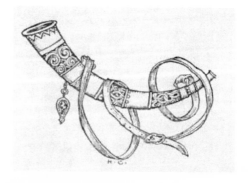

CHILDREN OF KINGS

MANY a stirring year had gone by since King Alfred told his story in Athelney, when it chanced upon a day that his little kinsman—now grown into a brave and stalwart man—rode through the vale of the White Horse, and bethinking him of his old nurse, turned aside to the village on the downs where she dwelt.

It was late in the spring-time. A warm light slept upon the hillsides; fruit-trees were flowering in the garth about the small log-house; a girl was singing half-hidden among the bright green leaves of the trees, and the prince checked his horse to listen to her.

For a moment as he stood at the doorway the old nurse gazed at him, wondering who he might be; then she caught him to her, laughing and crying; held him at arm's length and looked him fondly up and down. "Oh, little son of mine," she cried, "God has made you a tall man and strong; and good no less, I warrant. I little hoped to see you again, and now you bring me more joy than I can tell."

And when the horse had been put to graze in the meadow, she led him in and questioned him a hundred times of the king and of all her friends in the old days, and ran back in memory to his boyhood, asking him if he remembered this and that of the things done and said in the time long gone by. And when he in turn bade her tell him how she fared and if there was anything she needed for her happiness, "Nothing, dear lad," she answered, "unless it were to see you often, and to look once more, it might be, at the good king himself, were he to pass this way."

"And who is it sings so blithe among your apple-trees?" asked the prince.

"That is Egwina," said the nurse. "Her father was a shepherd on the downs, but he was lost in the snow of the Great Winter; and her mother died no long while after, so I brought her hither to be my foster-child."

"You had ever the big mother-heart, nurse," said the prince, "and little I wonder now at the flourish of your trees, for sweeter voice I never heard."

"Ay, and her face is as sweet as her voice, and her heart more sweet than either. But here is the garth. Will you not let her see what has come of the king's babe that lay in my lap?"

There then in the slumber of the ruddy sunshine these two met among the fruit-tree blossom, but red and white of apple and cherry were not more fresh and fair than the maid in her loveliness. And while Egwina thought, surely not even in the number of the king's great thegns is there any more lordly or more beautiful than this, the prince said to himself, here at last, by the blessed rood, I find the one girl in all the world that was meant for me.

So the prince wooed and won her; and when time had sped by, and their little son Athelstan had come to run about, a merry child with his mother's blue eyes and sunny hair, a new joy fell to Alfred's lot and he seemed to grow young again. Not that the king was now truly old, but illness and sorrow and many anxious labours had furrowed his brow and sown his hair with hoar-frost. Manly and cheerful he always was, but never more light of heart than when the boy was with him. Even while he conversed on learned matters with his Bishop Asser or dictated a book to John or Grimbold his Mass-priests, the little grandson would stand between his knees, holding his thumb, and waiting patiently till he could lure him away to some fresh revelry.

So dearly did the king love the child that when his sixth birthday came round, Alfred held a high feast at which he made him the youngest of his thegns. Calling him to the dais in the midst of the great chiefs, he buckled round him a sword-belt glittering with gems, threw a purple cloak over his shoulders, and drew back his long hair so that it fell down over the cloak in clusters of gold. Then he took a noble sword and held it out by the golden scabbard, and when the child grasped the hilt the king laughed gaily: "Aha, sea-rover! This time I have trapped you. You have taken the sword from me by the hilt, and that is a token that you are now my man."

"Yes, grandfather," Athelstan answered with a shining look, "always I shall be your man, and you shall be my man, and both of us shall man each other."

"So may it be!" rejoined the king. "And now I pray, little Stone of Nobleness, that you will wax as good as your name, ever remembering that goodness is the best nobleness, and that stone is the most steadfast thing in the world. And if some day God should make you king, I pray that He may be your strength against hardship and sorrow; for though there is not a king but would wish to be without these if he could, yet I know he cannot; so I do not pray that you may be quit of them. And God give you to know that every good gift and every power soon decays, and is heard of no more, if wisdom be not in it."

That, I think, was the happiest time in all the days of King Alfred's life, and it lasted to the end of it; for it was in that year, shortly before the Mass of All Hallows, that he died and was buried in the great church of the abbey he had founded at Winchester.

Long afterwards Athelstan came to the throne of his grandfather. He had waxed worthy of his name, as the king had prayed that he might do, and so well had he warded the land and kept faith with all men that his people called him the Steadfast. Looking abroad for some bright spirit of a man that he might make his friend, his thoughts turned to the north and rested upon Harald of the Fair Hair, who had subdued the hundred bickering little kings of the creeks and fells, and brought the whole of Norway under his strong rule. So it came about that on a summer evening as Harald feasted at Nidaros, an English earl entered the hall and strode up to the king's high seat, bearing a gift from Athelstan.

It was a sword of swords, fenced with a guard of gold and set in a gold sheath twinkling with precious stones. Harald rose graciously as he heard the message, but when the earl saw how he took the sword by the pommel, he laughed outright as King Alfred had laughed long years ago: "Aha, King of Norway, you have laid hand to hilt, so now you have made yourself King Athelstan's man."

Harald flushed and plucked the blade half from its sheath, and for a moment it seemed like as not that the jest would take an ill turn; but a happier thought flashed through his clear mind, and he answered with a smile: "That shall be as it may be. But the sword is a kingly sword, and it shall not cut kings' friendship. Sit on my right hand, Earl."

Now Harald's sons were a wild and turbulent brood, all save Hakon, the tricksy little elf of his old age, and he had often fretted lest, when he were gone, the child might fall into the hands of his fierce half-brothers. In this gift of the sword he saw a means of safety. "The boy shall go to England," he said, "and grow to his strength unharmed;" and as he planned all that was to be said and done in the matter, "That, I think, will be a jest worth two of the English earl's."

Next summer then, when Hakon was four years old, Hawk Halbrok and Sigurd the Earl bore away with him from Norway in two noble dragon-ships. Soon they saw the English shores running blue into the grey sea, and from them the sea-fowl came glittering; and up the broad reaches of Water of Thames they sailed between meadows smelling sweet of the summer; and where the tideway narrowed there were the flowery garths and white houses of London town. But most they wondered at the great bridge with its street of high gables across the river, and below it they moored to the rings of a wharf of stone.

Then thirty of the Norsemen sprang ashore with Hawk and Earl Sigurd—each with his sword hidden under his coat—and passed through the busy streets to the royal house. The king was sitting in council as they entered; and Hawk, who went foremost, bore the fair little lad on his left arm, and on his right he had heavy bracelets of gold, and he wore a crimson tunic, with his hair in a gold-embroidered silk cap. A strange gallant figure he made as he advanced straight to the king's throne, and without a word placed the boy upon the king's knee.

"What does this mean?" asked Athelstan, gazing in astonishment at the bold strangers.

"This is Harald Fair Hair's young son," answered Hawk, "that he has sent you to foster."

"Does he dare?" cried Athelstan, and his brows blackened with wrath, for the foster-father of another man's child was ever counted his inferior.

"You have the child set upon your knee, King," said Hawk, as he saw the fierce passion rising. "You may slay him if you will, but you will not have destroyed all the sons of Harald."

Athelstan glanced down at the boy, and the blithe little creature looked up into his face with eyes so fearless and friendly that the king's heart warmed towards him.

"Tell your King Harald I will keep his son. And setting babe against sword, it may be that he has sent me the goodlier gift."

Then said Earl Sigurd, "I am Harald's brother, and as he would not have you think we are come to you as beggars, he bade me pray you come down to our ships and see for yourself."

"Very willingly," answered the king.

Down to the quay they went straightway. One of the stately vessels was moored to the rings, but the other lay out in the stream. And never did ship more glorious swim on the Water of Thames; for forty rowers held it in its place against the race of the tide, and there it lay, with beak of gold, and dragon-coils of gold gleaming astern, shields of scarlet and silver to shelter the rowers on the benches, and glittering vane aloft on the masthead. From the great yard a purple sail hung billowing in the wind. Round it sailed the white swans that the folk of London loved to see on their river, and the salmon-fishers had crept up in their boats to behold the wondrous ship.

"This," said the earl, "is Harald's gift to you, King Athelstan; or, rather, I shall say, it is the casket that holds his gifts."

At a sign the rowers brought the vessel along-side the quay, and right gladly the king went on board.

In this fashion Hakon became Athelstan's foster-son. And the king had him baptised, and reared and taught with his own children; and he came to love him beyond words. So, indeed, did all people, for there was no lad more winsome in all England, or so tall and strong and comely as he.

Harald never saw his little elf again. His mighty heart broken by the ingratitude of his children, and all his fair hair white as snow, he died very old, and was laid in his cairn in Hordaland, with his war-gear about him. Under his son Erik peace or comfort in Norway there was none. His savage cruelty won him the name of Blood-axe, and when at last the people rose and drove out him and his wicked queen, Gunhild, King Athelstan equipped three war-ships for Hakon, girded him with Quern-biter (the Cutter of Millstones), and sent him forth glad and fearless to claim his royal heritage.

The lad had yet but turned his fifteenth year, and when the crowds at the Peasant Assembly saw him in the bloom of his boyish grace, their hearts went out to him; old men cried that 'twas Harald Fair

Hair come back young again; and quicker than fire glitters through dry grass, the tidings that he had been chosen king flew over Norway.

No one dreamed then of the adventure that lay before him. Nothing less was that than the overthrow of the ancient gods of the North; and a hopeless work Hakon found it to be. More than once did Sigurd, the stout heathen earl of his childhood, make peace between him and his unyielding people, but in those iron days kings were slow to learn that it was ill preaching the Gospel of Peace with fire and sword.

Yet for all his masterfulness, earl and peasant loved him well enough, and when the sons of Erik began their invasions, they upheld him staunchly by land and sea. But the Blood-axe brood brought him to his death at last. Under the wicked eyes of Brunhild herself, he had driven them in mad rout to their ships, when a random arrow struck him beneath his uplifted arm. His men carried him on board, and bent to their oars homeward. But life was ebbing fast, and Hakon was never to see home again. They turned aside and landed him on Hella, the Flat Rock, and there he died in the house in which he was born.

As the end drew near, his thoughts were busy with the country of Christ's earthly wayfaring; and thither, he said, he had a mind to go, if he lived, and be with Christian men. When he was asked whether he wished that his body should be taken to England, "Little better than a pagan have I lived in a pagan land," he answered; "bury me how you will."

So he too was laid kingly in his cairn by those true-hearted heathen folk; and Norway was ruled by another Harald, who was of the Blood-axe strain, and who was called Greyfell from the colour of his cloak.

So strangely do events repeat themselves, and from one generation to another weave together into a single picture the lives of men who were strangers to each other. Even beyond this the story goes. In the troubles that followed the death of King Hakon many of his friends and kinsfolk perished. Sigurd the wise and friendly earl was slain; and though Harald Grey Cloak proved a righteous king, and many of the people were brought to belief in Christ in his day, dearly did he abide that slaying, for the earl's son, Hakon, lured him to a treacherous death at last. Tryggva too, the under-king of Vikin, they killed in Christni Fjord; but his Queen, Astrid, escaped, and of that came many things worth telling.

OLAF THE VIKING

AFTER the slaying of Tryggva, Queen Astrid fled with a small following; and Thorold, her foster-father, led her through the dark pine woods and the rocky tracts of the fells to an island in a lonely lake, where she might safely lie hidden for a time. There her babe was born; and Thorold sprinkled him with water in the old heathen fashion, and called him Olaf after his grandfather. And as soon as the danger of pursuit appeared to have gone by, her little band of defenders returned quietly to their homes.

All through the summer the fair young queen remained on the island, nursing her little son, and hoping for happier fortunes. But as the red leaves began to fall, and the days to shorten and grow cold, "It is time now," said Thorold, "to get to your father's before the first snow." So they set out, Astrid and the babe, with two hand-maids, and Thorold and his son Thorgils, a boy of six years; and travelling by starlight, and keeping away from the homesteads except when it was late and dark, they arrived at Olfrusted and were in comfort there with her father during the winter.

Yet it was not long before a rumour of Olaf's birth reached the wicked old queen, Gunhild, and scarcely had the spring gales cleared the ice from the fjords and the snow from the passes before spies and troops of horsemen were sent out in search of the babe. "A little seed, son Harald, will tumble a stone wall," said Gunhild; "see that no bantling of the Fair Hair breed lives to shove you from your seat."

Then began a long and perilous flight through the Norland wilds of rock and water and forest; but neither on the wolf-pack's highway, which is the heathland, nor on the troll-wife's byway, which is the precipice, did any ill befall them, and foster-father Thorold brought them safely through into Sweden to the homestead of Hakon the Old.

Even to that shelter the hatred of Gunhild pursued them, but the kindly old king, knowing she was as treacherous as ice of one night's frost, made no more account of her gifts and promises than of her threats. "If Astrid will go with you, or give you the boy," he said to her messengers, "so let it be. For the rest, my old house lacks not silver, nor yet gold; no, nor good iron to take care of both." And when the messengers began to bluster, a grim thrall, glaring through his tangled red hair, sprang out upon them and drove them from the steading with his dung-fork.

For two winters they dwelt there in Sweden, and as the child grew ruddy and stout upon his feet, the old king said to him, "Now, comrade, none too early can we fit ourselves for the sport and work of great earls and warriors. Play with the harp-strings and the making of songs," he went on, laughing, "will come to thee later; but what should hinder thee in the summer-time from riding and steering and swimming—ay, and from the handling of sword and javelin in thy small way? Then in the winter we shall have the skates and the chessmen. And I think it may happen that thou shalt show some skill in the eight arts of the heroes while thy body is still supple and thy wits nimble. What sayst thou, little king's son?"

"He says he thanks thee, King Hakon," answered Astrid, drawing the lad to her knee, and looking across him to the old man with her young eyes shining; "and his mother thanks thee too. Often indeed I wonder, when I think of all the goodness we have had from thee. No other in these lands, I warrant, would have been so bold to befriend us as thou hast been."

Still, from time to time, came disquieting signs of the hatred and watchfulness of Gunhild, so that Astrid bethought her that the safest place for the child would be with her brother Sigurd, who was held in great honour by King Valdamar of Garda in the Russian land. Olaf had completed his third year when she spoke of this matter to Hakon the Old.

HE SAYS HE THANKS THEE, KING HAKON, ANSWERED
ASTRID...AND HIS MOTHER THANKS THEE TOO.

"I will not say thee nay," replied the king, "for it may be this is the wisest course. But oh, small companion-in-arms, I had thought thou wouldst stay to lay me in my cairn, and perchance to sit in my high seat after me. But Weird, who spins our thread of life, will have it otherwise. Well, well! it is much to remember that you two have been to me here in this house as pleasant as the morning-star and the red of the summer dawn, so that for the most part I have forgotten how all things for me are now drawing nigh to the end. Nay, do not look sad. Let us take all that comes to us with a cheerful heart. Merrily you shall depart, and seemly too, as befits folk dear to Hakon the Old."

He presented them with kingly gifts, gave them men and women servants, and put them in care of a company of worthy merchants faring eastward beyond the Baltic. But Garda they never reached, for their ship was captured by sea-rovers and carried in to Eistland. There Olaf saw his mother sold for a bond-woman and led away sorrowful; but he and Thorold and the lad Thorgils fell to the lot of a black-haired, beetle-browed Eistlander.

They were still standing on the quay when a yeoman came up, leading a fine goat. "What may be the price of the lads?" he asked the Viking. "Wilt thou take the goat in exchange for the two? The old man is of no use to me."

"A mouth to fill, and no use to any one," said the Eistlander; and raising his axe, he struck the old foster-father down, so that he fell dead into the wash of the sea.

"Friend, thou art quick," said the yeoman.

"Ay, 'twas ever word and blow with me," laughed the Viking. "Take the lads, and give me the goat."

But Olaf, with his little clenched fists crossed hard upon his breast, stood glaring at him.

"Wilt know me again?" said the Eistlander, scowling under his black brows.

"Ay," said Olaf, "that is not unlike."

So the lads passed from hand to hand in Eistland, till a farmer named Reas bought them. Olaf he never held for a thrall, but treated him as one of his own household, clad him handsomely, and reared him in all manly service. "Look at his long bright hair, wife," he said, "and his hands, and the fearless eyes and the proud bearing of him! A king's son he well may be, and at the lowest no less than some great earl's child."

"Clear enough it is to see," replied his wife gaily, "that there is nothing too good for him."

Now when Olaf had been for six years in the homestead with Reas, Sigurd, the brother of Queen Astrid, came west from Garda, collecting tribute for King Valdamar. As he rode into the garth at Reas-stead Olaf went forward to greet him and welcome his following. Sigurd gazed hard at the boy and asked him his name.

"My name is Olaf, son of Tryggva of Vikin."

"Then thy mother's name was Astrid, and so it chances that we are kinsmen," said Sigurd alighting; "for I am Sigurd, Astrid's brother."

"It was to thee then that we were sailing," said Olaf, "when the Vikings fell upon us;" and he told him of their evil fortune on sea and shore.

Then musing for a little while, Sigurd asked, "Wouldst thou be free and fare with me to Garda?"

"Ay, gladly enough, if Thorgils went free too."

"They are good lads," said Reas, when Sigurd questioned him, "and I had no thought to be rid of them; but if they wish to go with thee, thou shalt have them at a price and a promise."

"And what may that be?"

"For the elder a mark of gold is the price, but it is nine marks for this lad, for I will not say that I do not hold him dear."

"The more pleased am I to pay," replied Sigurd.

"And this is the promise," Reas went on; "thou shalt treat them well; they shall not be sold again; and if thou wouldst be rid of them thou shalt bring them back to me."

"That I think will not happen," said Sigurd, "for this is my sister's child."

With warm leave-taking and many a look backward the lads rode out from Reas-stead, and so with Sigurd to Holmgard, which is Great Novgorod in the Russian realm.

Now it happened on a day in Holmgard that as Olaf wandered among the folk at the fair there were men sitting by a stall, and as he passed them he heard one say, "Wise men think before they speak, but thou art as ready with thy hand as with thy tongue." "Ay," laughed another, "'twas ever word and blow with me!"

At the sound of the voice Olaf drew the axe from his belt, and for an instant he saw again, as if it were happening before him, the good old man fall dead into the wash of the sea. He turned about sharp. There sat the Eistlander, with the braggart laugh still on his brute mouth; and Olaf, springing forward, buried his axe between his beetling brows, and fled.

"I have slain a man," he panted, as he burst in upon Sigurd.

"Then, kinsman," said Sigurd drily, "it is like enough that thou wilt soon lose thy life."

"Thou wouldst have slain him thyself," cried Olaf; "'twas he that killed Thorold, thy sister's foster-father, as I told thee."

"Ay?" replied Sigurd; "then I will not say but that things might have been worse. We must away to the queen, and that quickly. It may be that she will, of her grace, stand between thee and the law."

Now when Queen Olga saw the fair lad and heard all that had befallen during his brief life, she laid her hand gently on his sunny head. "Pity it were," she said, "that one so young and comely, and a king's son, should lose his life in such a case." And summoning her guard, she gave him into their safe-keeping; and when the matter had been brought before King Valdamar, she paid his blood-fine for the slaying of the Eistlander. So Olaf laid his hands between the queen's and became her man.

Here now was he who had been bartered and sold for a thrall come at last to a great house, where the benches were wrought of walrus tusks, and the white swan smoked on the board, and the silver cups were crowned with sweet mead and green wine. So strangely up and down does Fortune turn her wheel!

Proud and stirring days were these for Olaf among the queen's warriors, who took him for their comrade-in-arms and luck-bringer. Many a ringing song and wild tale set his heart beating and his eyes gleaming as he listened to their talk of adventure by land and sea. They told of Viking fights along the shores of the Baltic, and of rich spoil to be won in the green islands away sunsetward; of the leagues of black pine-forest and the tracks over which ships were hauled on wheels to the mighty rivers flowing into the South; but most of all he delighted to hear of the huge mysterious mounds on the steppe, where old Scythian kings were said to be buried between sheets of pure gold, and of the wondrous city Miklagard (Byzantium or Constantinople), where the wharves were of white marble, and great vessels rested their gilded prows against the houses while their sterns were afloat.

When Olaf was twelve years old and had grown very tall and strong, Queen Olga gave him three ships, and sent him forth on his first cruise against the lands and cities which had broken away from Garda and refused tribute. Goodly sailers they were, with scarlet hulls, and beaks carved in scarlet and gold, black oars, and gilt vanes, and white sails striped with blue and green. Since Olaf was in command and was of royal blood, he was called king, according to the custom in Garda; and nothing less than kingly was his bearing, in his mail-shirt of woven rings, with his long yellow hair clustering on his fringed red cloak, and the bright look of good fortune on his face. That autumn he brought home much tribute and plunder, gold and silver, fine raiment, and costly work in amber and jet, ivory, and precious stones.

So through the blithe summers Olaf went sea-faring, and ever as the moon of hunters rose red and ruddy over the forest, his ships drove into Holmgard laden with booty, and Queen Olga received him with a gracious welcome. King Valdamar soon made him war-lord of his frontiers, and the seers and wise men declared that guardian spirits, of a more shining aspect than any seen before, had come with the young stranger into the land.

But some of the great folk about the court were bitter with envy, and they tried to fill the king's mind with suspicions and fears. "It is easy," they said, "to make any man powerful, but when he is powerful, is it easy to keep him true?" "If a stranger mocks the old gods of any land, the evil may fall not upon him but upon the land that suffers him." But most of all they feared lest Olaf should sow division between their lord and the queen.

Sigurd heard rumours of these plots and warned Olaf, but when Valdamar looked into the lad's frank face his doubts and fears vanished. Of the ancient gods indeed Olaf took little heed, and when the king reproached him, he answered, "No great joy, I think, King Valdamar, comes to you of their worship; for as often as you visit them I see your look, which is kingly and gracious, grown dark and heavy with care. And let not dread of their anger trouble you, for being gods they must now know whither I shall ride or sail in the new spring;" and straightway he begged the king leave to depart, "though whether southward by the forests and Mother Dneiper to Miklagard, or westward to the great seas, I cannot tell."

And half relieved and half reluctant, Valdamar consented.

Upon a night when the spring was at hand and the sweet gales of a new time sang through the pine-woods and rocked the broken ice on the sea-ways, Olaf saw in a dream a pillar of stone that ascended into the heavens; and it was so notched with foot-holds that he began to climb. Ever upward he went until he had passed through the clouds, and beheld around him wide fields of summer flowers. The fragrance was more sweet than that of any earthly wind, and among the flowers walked joyful people clad in white. Beside him he heard the voices of two unseen who spoke concerning him: "He hath not bowed down to idols of wood and stone, and if he doth not worship Thee, it is that he hath not known Thee;" and the other answered, "In a little while the winds of the world shall bear him to the place where he shall know me, and he shall learn to strive after righteousness." Then as Olaf descended into the clouds, he heard the lamentation of men despairing; and far beneath, in the shadow of the nether fires, he saw the shapes of the ancient gods sitting in chains, and the wraiths of their worshippers—mighty chiefs of the cairns that overlook the sea, and forgotten kings who had been buried between sheets of gold. And he awoke trembling and in great awe.

Thus came the gallant days of Holmgard to an end; and all that summer Olaf raided fjord and bay, and chased the sails of viking and chapman to the westward; but when the weather broke he ran for safe anchorage under the lee of Wendland, where Geira, the daughter of King Burislaf, was queen. When she was told of his coming she sent messengers begging him to pass the winter with her. "Very willingly," said Olaf, and had his ships laid snug in a sheltered nook and tented over against wind and snow.

Right glad of each other were these two when they met, for although Geira was a widow, there was no woman more beautiful in Wendland, and she and Olaf were of one age. Before Yule-tide came they were married; and in the stately house with them was Astrid, her young sister, who loved Olaf dearly. Speedily he brought the realm to peace and strong rule, harrying robber-holds and quelling lawless towns, which had set the queen at nought in the days of her widowhood.

For three winters Olaf abode in Wendland, and near the close of the third it happened that they sat in hall upon a night when snow drifted and the wind blew keen through cranny and crevice. The tapestry shook along the walls; and as the light of the pine-logs flickered over it, and the figures wrought in it seemed to be alive, Gizur the poet touched his harp and made songs of the pictures— merry songs and mournful, songs of yesterday and of long ago, love songs and sword songs and songs of ships sinking. But after he had ceased Geira sat buried in thought; and when Olaf asked why she was so silent, "Once," she answered, "these men and women were as happy as we, and as glad to be living; but now they are all dead, and scarce remembered. Of all their dear lives there is left but a working in coloured threads, and little we think of it, except as a screen to keep the wind away."

It was not long thereafter that Geira fell sick and died. When she was gone, it was as though the sun had set in darkness in midsummer, and no warm glow lingered through the night on the brown lakes and the pine-forest. He went out and sat on a blue stone, gazing blindly across the green nesses and the grey seas; and Astrid knelt in front of him, and held his hand between hers. And when he rose up, roaring with the dumb pain of his heart, she stood beside him, but spoke no word, for she knew that sorrow lay heavy upon him. Then he looked at her, and put his arms about her head: "Little girl, there is no delight now in Wendland!"

And going down to the shore, he bade the men make the ships ready for sea.

About this time Lodin, a rich merchant of Vikin, came to a place in Eistland where a fair was being held, and among the thralls who stood for sale he saw a woman, and though she was meanly clad and wasted and wan, he recognised her for the wife of King Tryggva. He questioned her, and when she had told him all the ills that had befallen her, "Take heart again, lady," he said. "Thy little son, as I have heard, has grown to a name renowned among kingly men, and I wot he has long looked for thee in vain. But come now, wilt thou not plight me thy troth and let me take thee back with me to thine own land?" The poor queen's heart was full, and she bowed her head in consent; and this was the end of her sorrows.

But Olaf sailed westward, with never a glance thrown back to Wendland. So widely had his fame spread that as he swept into Eyra-sound, Sweyn of the Forked-beard, gathering his crews for the summer raiding, would not suffer him to pass, but must needs have him for his guest. When their friendship had somewhat grown, "What blither sea-ranging would you have," asked the Dane, "than to put your ships to mine, and share with me this harrying of England?" "None blither, perchance," said Olaf; "and if you would have it so, you should find me no laggard." So, with a humming wind in the shrouds, the summer-host of the kings goes churning the bath of the wild swans.

Now we are in England; and the sea-warden on the cliffs, and the fisher in the bay, and the shepherd on the links see the ships go by — ninety sail and three; and a flock of ravens follows them in the sunset. Riders and runners speed along the coast, and at dusk signal-fires break out on the hill-tops. But where the Vikings land they find few in thorp or farmstead to withstand them, until they came to Maldon Blackwater.

Swiftly they crowded into the bay; and, ship after ship, their coloured sails dropped as the keels grounded on the long low isle in the midst of the Panta river. From Maldon town on the ridge Earl Brytnoth rode down with the men of Essex to meet them; but the tide was at the flood and the water ran deep between the two hosts. Then to the further side of the stream came a herald from the ships, and cried with a mighty voice, "Hail and hearken; these are the words of the sea-rovers. Hasten, men of the land, with the price of your safety. Better that silver and gold should defend you than that we should meet in the rush of spears. If you, lord and leader, will agree to redeem your people, the Vikings will give you friendship; peace they will make with you, and taking the tribute on board, turn again seaward."

Brandishing his lance aloft, Brytnoth sent his words ringing across the water: "Take back the answer of this people. Here stand we for the king and the realm, for homestead and kinsfolk. Take back the answer of Brytnoth. Look well at the tribute we bring. For gold you shall have spear-heads, and the keen edges of swords for silver. Thus far have you come unfought, but you go unfought no further."

Then, to and fro, whistled flights of arrows until the ebbing tide ran shallow upon the ford, which went on a narrow ridge of rock through the deep waters of the Patna stream. The Vikings thronged down to the bank, with eager shouts to press forward; but Brytnoth bade Wulfstan hold the passage with Elfhere and Maccus, and the rovers who ventured out upon that sunken bridge fared on a longer journey than they had thought to take.

When the ship-folk saw how warily the track was guarded, they challenged Brytnoth with scoffing cries: "Meet us as heroes meet, hand to hand on open ground. Come over to us here on the isle, or give us way to you across the ford." The proud earl drew back his defence, and answered scornfully, "Take your passage without toll, and here is room on the shore for many graves!"

Too much English earth did the great-heart that day in his disdain give away to strangers.

Then flew the ravens in circles over the rush of spears, and Dane and Saxon closed in the crimson fight of Maldon Blackwater.

For many a year afterwards gleemen sang of it, and round the bivouac fire and in the thegn's hall men's hearts leaped to the battle-cry, "Stand fast for king and country!" Never doubt that Olaf and the Forked-beard were in the forefront of that onset, but the maker of the old song had no care for the names of any but his own English folk.

Struck by a rover's spear, Brytnoth snapped the shaft with his shield, and thrust his foeman through the throat. With a second deadly cut he rent another's ring-mail asunder, and, laughing for gladness, thanked God for the good day's work He had given him to do. This way and that swayed the fight as young men and veterans fell; and now the Danes gave way, and now the Saxon ranks were borne backward.

In one fierce charge the earl was pierced through with an assagai—such was the name of the keen outland weapon. A stripling who fought by his side drew it from the gushing wound, and hurling it back, slew the sender. "A gallant cast, son of Wulfstan!" cried Brytnoth, unsheathing his axe as a tall fair-haired Viking pressed in upon him; but before the old hero could strike, a sea-wolf hewed down his arm. The broad brown axe dropped from his grasp; he could hold it no longer. Still his voice rang out cheerily, "Stand fast, East Saxons, stand fast!" And at length when he felt his feet failing under him, he looked up to heaven and prayed aloud: "Lord of all folk, from a full heart I thank Thee for all the delight I have had in this world, for the love of woman and the bliss of little children, for the fellowship of true men, for home and gear, for service and honour, for long life and the strong arm, for this goodly land and glad sea, for all the fair world of Thy making. And not least I thank Thee for this seemly death. Now, Lord of clemency, grant my spirit grace in my need; take it, Lord of angels, in peace to Thy safe-keeping."

Scarcely had he ceased when the heathen smote him to the earth, and spoiled him of his arms and bracelets; and at his side fell the stripling Wulfmer, son of Wulfstan the ford-warden.

The hedge of shields was broken. Dastards turned and fled; but the great-hearts of Essex—Edward the Long, Elfwine, Offa, and many another—fought shoulder to shoulder, and died about the body of Brytnoth.

"Too old am I for wayfaring," said Brytwold the hoary; "here I stay, and to-night I think to sleep beside the lord and comrade I loved."

Escferth, the Northumbrian hostage, said nothing, but listened well-pleased to the creaking of his great bow as he sped arrow after arrow into the pack of the sea-wolves.

Thus the old hero-song leaves them fighting by the Panta stream, below the grey earthworks of Maldon; the last page of it has been lost; how the Saxon gleeman brought it to a close has long been forgotten.

Through the deep woods and along the reedy water-lanes of the Fens the body of Brytnoth was borne by the monks to the minster at Ely. Far across marsh and mere floated their dirge-music as they laid it to rest before the high altar in the choir.

"Above all men I have known," said the abbot, "this lord was strong and gracious. Great-hearted he was and glad-hearted, a true thegn of Christ, courteous and loyal to the humblest. Long shall I bear in mind his last message to me, 'Tell my Lord Abbot that I cannot dine without my men, because I cannot fight without them.' Such an earl we cannot look to have again."

But a coward fear of the sea-rovers fell upon King Ethelred and his councillors. They kissed the hand that smote them; they fed the marauders who pillaged them; they bought a shameful peace. Ten thousand pounds of silver was weighed out from the treasure chests and taken down in waggons to the ships.

When the kings had divided the spoil, Sweyn bore away to Denmark, but Olaf, as you shall hear, spread his white sails striped with blue and green down the track of the westering sun.

OLAF IN ENGLAND

BITTER cause had folk to remember those white sails striped with blue and green, for Olaf cruised along Frankland, plundering town and village; and doubling the red granite horns of Brittany, ran down the rich sunny coast until the snow-capped mountains of Spain stretched east and west before him, like the outermost wall of the world.

"I have heard of these mountains," said Leif, son of Eric the Red, whom he had with him on that voyage. "Bear away to the south-west, and we shall come to the Long Sea, and the burning land of the Blackamoors, and Rome the Golden City of old time."

Coming at last to Italy they saw the hills green with vines and grey with olives, and a fair white city glittering on the shores of a blue bay. They dropped sails far out in the offing and planned to steal to land in the dark and capture the place at daybreak. That night they feasted on a sea of stars with a starry heaven over them; but in the dark hour before dawn, as they glided across the bay with a cautious dip of the oars, suddenly innumerable bells began to ring out along the shore—bells loud and clear, bells faint and far away; and lights gleamed out red from the darkness, in the city, on the shore, among the vineyards and olive groves, as if the whole land had sprung up from sleep. They ceased rowing, and as they hung on their oars in amazement, they heard the distant voices of people calling and answering each other.

Scared by that strange awakening, the rovers put out to sea again, little thinking it was the matin bells summoning to prayer the holy men and women whose convents were thickly scattered on the hills, that had saved the city from pillage.

They had but few such mischances, and such booty fell to their daring as had never yet been seen in Norland waters. Rich raiment there was, and silks and cloth of gold, Greek ewers and basins set with jewels, swords and gilt armour, chalices and crosses rough with gems, and caskets of carved ivory containing gold-lettered Gospels written on purple vellum.

In the third year after Maldon fight they turned their dragon-prows to the west, and as they fared homeward old Harald Blue-tooth died, so that Sweyn became sole king in Denmark. And Sweyn held a great funeral feast at which he drank to the memory of his father, and took an oath to harry England again ere the summer was over and tumble Ethelred from his throne. Then the huge ale-horns were drained to the memory of Christ, and the third rouse they gave to St. Michael. Not long thereafter Sweyn and his host got to their ships, and meeting with Olaf in the North Sea, both kings steered for England.

In many a field the harvesters toiled in the hot sun till all the corn was cut and bound in sheaves, save a patch in the centre. At last that too was cut at a stroke; the men planted their scythes upright and clashed their whetstones and the long blades thrice together. The women emptied the crumbs from their baskets; the men spilt a sup of ale on the field, drank deep, and waved their hats, cheering. Then all went singing to the farmstead, while the sparrows swung on the straggling stalks left standing for the little elves.

Scarcely had the harvest been gathered in when the Viking fleet rose like a pageant from the sea. Four-and-ninety sail, they crowded up the Thames to burn London, but it was the Latter Ladymas, and, with our Lady's help, the townsfolk beat them back. Then the rovers swarmed into creeks and river-mouths, and getting horses from burning village and farm, went plundering and man-slaying from Thanet to the Hampshire woods.

Once again Ethelred opened his treasure-chests and paid sixteen thousand pounds of silver for a hollow peace. The price of that ignominy would have bought the whole of Kent, water and weald.

So Sweyn lay at Southampton, with the West Saxons to victual his people for the winter if he were minded to stay; but Olaf was bent on a haven further west under the warm headlands of Devon. Before they parted came tidings of a mighty sea-fight in Norway. "And this matter, I think," said Sweyn, "concerns you nearly, for it is time such a man as you are should remember the old kingliness of his race."

Now the news told of a venture of the Jomsborg Vikings to wrest Norway from Hakon, the son of Earl Sigurd. With sixty ships they sped northward, plundering and slaying, and Hakon met them with one hundred and fifty in Hiorunga Bay. Then the fleets closed in the grimmest of sea-fights; but the Jomsborg vessels were the larger and taller, and so fast and fierce the Vikings shot that Hakon's men gave way. Faint hope was there of his winning in that strife; and when he saw his ships drifting loose, full of the dead and the dying, he took his little son, Erling, a lad of seven years, and sacrificed him to the fierce goddess of the Hell-grove. Black grew the heavens with storm; giant hail drove in the faces of the Vikings, the sea hissed and whitened. In the midst of the sudden tumult a woman was seen on the bows of Hakon's ship darting flashes of death from each hand. The Vikings cut their lashings and fled; some were captured, others escaped to the open sea. The earl's power was unbroken.

The land had sunken again to paganism. Hakon had brought back the dread gods of the old time, with their evil worship and cruel sacrifices. Of these things the people made little account, but as the earl grew grey, he had grown the more wicked and wanton, till there was no man or woman safe from the waywardness of his dark soul.

Thinking of these strange chances, Olaf sailed away, but ere he reached Devon great gales caught his ships and drove them far out of their course, and when the weather abated they were near the Scilly Isles, and put in there for water. Upon a rock in that wild cluster of islands dwelt a hermit, who was said to have the far-sight of things to come and to behold the lives of men as in a magic glass. Thereto he knew the speech of birds, and the island folk did not doubt but that the gulls and petrels, the terns and grey lag geese brought him the rumours of far-off lands, so that he foretold little that did not come to pass.

Many of the rovers were eager to look upon him, and to learn, if they might, what luck should befall them.

"Let us put his craft to the trial," said Olaf. "Thorolf shall take my name and go in my stead, and perchance we shall make merry over what comes of it."

Whereupon it was "Out oars!" and away to the Hermit's Rock. The seamen found the holy man seated at the mouth of his cave, and they perceived that he was tall and large of limb, but exceeding aged. They stayed their oars and called aloud, "Here comes the king to speak with thee," but they got no answer.

Thorolf leaped ashore in gold-inlaid helmet, bright sark of mail, and gold-fringed cloak of scarlet, of all the rovers the tallest and handsomest save Olaf himself. Still the hermit never moved from the stone, and it was not till the Viking stood beside him that he raised his eyes. They were blue and cold, and for the first time Thorolf knew what it was to be afraid.

"Did you think to make a mock of me?" asked the seer. "You are not the king. Yet, since you have come, I give you this warning, Be true to your king. Go back now the way you came."

Then Olaf himself, greatly wondering, came to the isle, and the hermit standing on the brink of the sea greeted him with outstretched hand, "Welcome, fair son!" and leading him to his cave, questioned him of his seafaring and of his early years.

"And this is your home?" asked Olaf, as the old man paused for a moment in thought. "A lonely spot it is for any one."

"Not so lonely as it seems to you," replied the hermit. "Where a man is, there is his angel, though mortal eyes may often see him no more than one sees the clear air. And Christ doth not forget us. Nor is the High King of heaven ever far from any of us. Here, too, be many birds, both of the sea and of the ancient land, and gentleness makes them tame. Also the seals come hither, and they have no fear."

"But a man needs the fellowship of his like."

"That is so," said the hermit, "and the folk of these isles are kindly neighbours. They come to me, and I go to them, when the heart calls;" and he showed Olaf in the depths of the cave his coracle of beast skin stretched over a wicker frame-work.

"And has this ever been your home?" then, laughing, he added quickly, "A child's question, I think."

"Nay, in my youth," replied the aged man, "I was such a one as yourself, full of delight in adventure and strife, full of the pride of strength, and the wild joy of the earth. I thought I had forgotten it all. Strange how your Norland eyes and fair hair bring back days long gone by. I remember tall men of your country. They came to London town yonder with wondrous ships and a four-year-old child; "and he told the story of Athelstan's foster-son, who came to be a great king.

"Ay, Hakon," said Olaf; "my father was kinsman of his, and ruled for him in Vikin, as I have said."

"Little it profits to recall those days of the roving eyes and the wayward heart. Fifty years hath God sustained me in these isles, a sinful man, for His high purpose. But come and see what I would show you."

The holy man led Olaf by a rugged path to the summit of his rock.

"Look around on these many isles, little and large, sown by the score on these bright waters."

Some of them were bare spires and shelves of stone on which only sea-birds could perch; others were still gaily coloured with grass and wild flowers; here and there, on the largest, blue smoke rose from the fisher-women's fires, and near them rode his own ships.

"From of old," said the hermit, "the folk have called them Scilly, the Isles of the Sun. And in truth they are the mountain peaks and plateaus of an ancient land where that bright light of the heavens was worshipped. Now it is sunken deep and lost, like a great ship gone down at sea. So say the ancient winter tales, and I believe them. Could you but raise this sunken land up from the dark gulfs, what a realm it would be for your kingship!"

Olaf gazed at the speaker in astonishment, but the holy man continued: "I know you would ask me of the hidden things that are to happen. This I will tell you. You shall come to great glory and power, and shall be a mighty king. And this shall be the work appointed to you; not to heave up valleys and mountains out of the sea, but to raise a people sunken in darkness and the worship of evil spirits. You shall make known to them the Lord Christ, whom you yourself know not yet; and that land you shall lift up to the true Sun."

Then the hermit stretched his arm towards the isles. "There lie your ships," he said; "goodlier have I never seen, with their gilded beaks and coloured shields. This token I give you that you may believe my words. You shall not sail far from this before you shall do battle. Men shall be slain on this side and that, and you sorely wounded. Yet in seven nights you shall be well again; and thereafter you shall accept the true faith and holy baptism."

AND THAT LAND YOU SHALL LIFT UP TO THE TRUE SUN.

It all came to pass as the aged man foretold, for out upon the high seas the rovers fell into hot contention, and Thorolf with three ships broke away from Olaf, and attacked him. Thorolf and six tall men were slain in the fight and buried in the cold sea; but Olaf, who had been stricken hard with an arrow, was taken by his men to an island where there was a great minster. As they bore him ashore on his shield, he saw the brethren come to meet him, with their abbot in white robes and cloth of gold, which glittered a long way off in the sun. They bade him welcome, and leading the way to their cloister, bound up his wound with precious balsam, so that in seven nights he was healed.

Much he communed with the Abbot Bernard and questioned him of the hermit, and of the White Christ, and the true faith. At nights, as Olaf and his people sat at their ale, the abbot told them of the life and death of God's Son on earth. Like little children they listened, and when they had heard that wondrous saga, they cried out, "We will be Christ's men," and consented to be baptised. Out of his spoil Olaf gave the abbot costly gifts, cross and chalice set with gems, rich vestments, and a golden Gospel.

Thereafter he sailed to Southampton. Sweyn Forked-beard had departed, but Elphege the bishop came from Winchester to visit him. The two rode to Andover, where Ethelred received them with much honour, and Olaf promised the king that he would never again harry England. That winter the ships were drawn up on the shore of the great haven under the Hampshire woods, and Olaf abode in peace, a Christian man in a Christian land.

All through the cold months one thought was in Olaf's mind—how he should fare to Norway, overthrow the wicked Earl Hakon, and get mastery of all the realm that had been Harald Fair Hair's. He talked over these things with Bishop Sigurd, and planned how he should take priests and monks with him, and first they should hie to Dublin and learn from the merchants and shipmen, who trafficked there in those days, what the folk were saying and doing in Norway.

So when the new spring came and fair weather, he put again to sea and came to the Green Isle. It chanced upon a day, as the ships lay off the coast, that the rovers came back from a foray with many hundred head of cattle, and among them the cows of a poor peasant. The wretched old carle hurried after them, and besought the king to have pity on his misery. "Pick out thy cattle from the drove if thou canst," said Olaf, "but we cannot be stayed by thee."

"Thy bed be in the heavens, king," said the man and turning to the dog that was with him, "Fetch them out, Vigi," he cried.

The dog was a big shaggy creature, brown and black in colour, and he ran this way and that among the horned beasts, and got the cows together.

"The brand on each of them, as thou seest, king, is the same."

"Ay," replied Olaf, "the beasts are surely thine." Then stroking the dog's head, "Wilt thou part with this wonderful Vigi?" he asked.

"To thee, king, very gladly, for thou wilt use him well."

"Great thanks," said Olaf; and drawing a coil of gold from his arm, he gave it to the old man, "Let this be a token of friendship between us."

After a sharp look at his old master's face, Vigi went readily on board, and no comrade had Olaf truer to the end than this great dog.

Now the fame of these Viking raids and the golden spoils spread over Norway; and when it was said that this Oli of Garda (for so Olaf had named himself) was of the line of the Norland kings, Earl Hakon was disquieted and took counsel of his friend, Thori Klak. "If this be the son of Tryggva," he said, "I look for hard fighting ere long, and little good to come of it. Now, Thori, to Dublin I would have you go and discover the truth in this matter. Should it prove as I misdoubt it will, make friends with this Olaf and lead him with bright hopes that, if he returns with you, the folk will surely rise against me and choose him for king. But if you cannot bring him into my hands, find a way to slay him." Olaf's uncles, too, Jostein and Karlhead, the brothers of Queen Astrid, he forced by threat of torture to go with Thori and bear out his tale.

A lucky day it seemed to Olaf when he got to Dublin and met his own kinsmen among the Norland folk. Eagerly he questioned them, and brighter omens of success could not be wished for than Thori's talk of how things had gone from bad to worse with Hakon, so that any change would be better for the people than this earl's masterful wickedness. But since the overthrow of the Jomsborg Vikings who was there daring enough to cope with him?

"Perchance a man of Harald Fair Hair's lineage," said Olaf, "and he not far away from us who are speaking here."

"That," cried Thori joyfully, "will be welcome news in Norway."

So out of Dublin Bay, and northward by the Western Isles, Olaf sailed with five ships to the realm of his kinsfolk. The plotters, in their own ship, bore him company; and as they stretched away from the Orkney Islands it was high summer.

AT STRIFE WITH THE GODS

OUT of the summer sea heaved the rugged blue summits of Norway. The ships put in to Moster Haven, and Bishop Sigurd joyfully sang mass in the king's tent. Thori, however, grew anxious lest the news of Olaf's coming should stir the people to a sudden uprising against the earl, and he urged the king to act secretly and to hasten northward night and day. "Thy best chance," he said, "is to fall upon Hakon without warning. If thy name be noised abroad and thou give him time to gather his strength, little luck, I think, will go with thy venture." Crafty though this counsel was, no other could have served Olaf's turn better.

Again the bright sails bellied to the wind, and leaving the sheltered sea-way along the rocky walls of the coast, the ships skirted the outer isles of the broken chain of rocks and skerries which stretches away to the north.

Hour after hour Olaf watched in silent gladness the slowly changing outlines of the wild realm which he claimed for Christ. The long day declined, but the light of a setting sun which never wholly set flushed the restless sea and the hushed heavens with a slumbrous glow wherein the stern mountains, the jagged reefs, and the billows that broke upon them appeared transformed into a world overgrown with flowers. It was a world too in which there was no sound except the low murmuring of wind and water.

In the stillness and the strange beauty of that sun of the night, it seemed to Olaf for a moment as though he were sitting once more on the blue stone beside the sea in Wendland and that Geira had just died. All the radiance and joy of existence had gone out with the light of her eyes; but now for the first time since her death the earth was again clothed with magical colour and sweetness. Sorrow fell away from him. He felt no longer the ache of bereavement or the hopelessness of regret. His spirit sprang up young and confident, and with a mind free from care he stood at the beginning of a new life. "Thanks and praise to Christ," he said, "I am my own man again. Henceforth I fare onward without grief or misgiving."

One by one, through the glamour of the summer night, the six ships sailed northward, as silent as ships in a dream.

It was close upon midnight, and Bishop Sigurd stood at Olaf's side. Of the sunken sun only an arc remained, burning blood-red between the purple sea and a green sky dappled with dull crimson and gold; and a track of fire ran across the rolling waves.

"We stand between night and morning," said Olaf. "Another day begins, and another time."

"Pray God's blessing on it," rejoined the bishop, "for a mighty work lies before you, and more dangerous enemies oppose it than perchance you dream of."

As he uttered the words faint strains of an unearthly music floated to them from some unknown distance in sea or air. Olaf gazed intently and then pointed to the far heavens. Dimly visible at first, a strange wedge-shaped shadow passed among the softly coloured clouds. As it advanced it grew darker and vaster, but glimmerings of light played upon it, and the faint strains of music changed into clear trumpet-notes ringing down from the sky.

"It is the singing swans," said Olaf. "See how the great flock whitens as it comes nearer. Listen, and you will hear the strange beating of their wings."

"Domine Deus!" cried Sigurd, signing himself with the cross; "these are not swans; and their voices are singing human words."

"No," replied Olaf in awestruck tones; "they are Odin's maidens, the Choosers of the Slain. Thus, it is said, they sing their song of death as they hasten to some battle-field."

"Nay, son, this is but an illusion of the Spirit of Evil," said the bishop, as the spectral host swept overhead and their garments streamed in white and dusky folds with the speed of their flight.

"Look," exclaimed the king, "look at the sun!"

Near the blood-red arc and against the light of the green sky moved awful and colossal shapes, which were luminous at one moment and at the next seemed to be wild and menaceful shadows.

"I know not how I know," whispered Olaf, "but those are the ancient gods of the land."

The bishop did not answer, but his lips moved in prayer: "*Adveniat regnum tuum*—Thy kingdom come; Thy will be done in earth as it is in heaven."

Out of the distance came a fierce cry as of the wind in winter: "Return, return, ere we slay you, troublers of the land!"

But the ships sailed on in silence.

Then a great flash of lightning split the heavens with rifts of flame, and a peal of thunder rolled along the deep. Flash followed flash, and in the dazzling brightness the giant shapes of the old gods were seen to be in swift commotion, coming across the sea.

Olaf snatched his sword from its scabbard, caught it by the blade, and held the cross high above his head. The jewelled hilt and the white blade glittered in the lightning. Clear to see also were the gold helmet, the steel ring-shirt, and the crimson mantle of the king. Then in a pause of the thunder Olaf cried back his answer: "With Christ to aid me, I take up thy challenge, Thor!"

WITH CHRIST TO AID ME, I TAKE UP THY CHALLENGE THOR.

In an instant the tumult ceased. The dread shadows vanished. The red sun rose half out of the sea, and the slumbering glow quickened towards day.

Sigurd and the king gazed at each other in wonderment.

"Are these—things that we have seen?" asked Olaf; "or was it all a dream and phantasm of the night?"

"What we have seen, many have seen," replied the bishop, with a wide movement of his hand.

Then Olaf became aware of crowds of faces on the ships turned towards him in silent inquiry, for a great awe had fallen on the men, and they marvelled how the mighty gods of the ancient days had been abashed and scattered by the vision of the cross and the name of Christ.

When they had come to Agad Ness, Thori persuaded the king to abide there until he returned with tidings of the earl's movements and the temper of the people. "Thus," he said, "you will best choose the course that it will be wisest to follow." So they cast anchor and lay in quiet that day under the Ness in Drontheim Fjord.

Late in the evening the traitor came back in haste and called Jostein and Karlhead to him. "Things," he said, "have taken a turn that is little to my liking; we must do what we may to amend them." And when he had taken counsel with them he bade them bring Olaf ashore to confer with him in secret.

The two rowed to the king's ship, and as they came alongside the king was leaning on the rail as though he awaited them, and Vigi lay at his feet.

"Thori has returned," said Karlhead; "he has sent to ask thee if thou wilt come ashore and speak with him unobserved."

"Ay," said Olaf, and without more ado he went over the rail and dropped into the boat. The great dog tried to follow him, but Olaf bade him lie down and be still. He paid no heed, and ran to and fro whimpering and whining; and when the boat had been pushed off he uttered a woeful howl, and springing into the fjord began to swim after them.

They had not taken many strokes when Jostein cried, "Where is thy sword, king? How is it thou art weaponless?"

Olaf's hand moved quickly to his empty belt, and he shook his head with a smile. "Even the most careful forget at times," he answered.

"The king must not go unarmed," rejoined Jostein; "we will row back for thy sword."

"Give way, friends! Kings are ever armed," said Olaf. As the men sat motionless, hesitating what to do, Olaf's eyes rested on the eager face of the dog swimming. "Let us take the poor creature on board," he said. "'Tis hard to punish him for being faithful."

He stretched out his hand and patted his head before lifting him into the boat. "Good soul, thou hast a woman's love in thy shaggy body! Now, kinsmen, give way!"

But the two still rested on their oars, and the warm glow of the summer night tinged the island rocks, and the ruddy reflection of these lit up the waters of the fjord.

"Would it surprise thee, king," at last Karlhead asked slowly, "to hear that the yeomen have risen in arms against Hakon? The war-arrow with its twisted cord has been sent round. The dissolute old madman is in hiding among the hills, but all the countryside is searching for him. His ships are waiting for him in the creeks, but they will not be able to save him."

"These indeed are tidings!" cried Olaf. "Thori's counsel was wise. Why do we waste time here?"

"Listen to the end," said Jostein. "Do not think too hardly of us, sister's-son. It was not our good will to seek thee out in Dublin and lure thee hither. It was that, or death and torture, for us."

"How should you lure me?"

"Thori swore to bring thee and deliver thee to Hakon, or if that should fail, to slay thee off the earth."

"Ay? And that was Thori's thought. And what would Thori do now?"

"When we have landed he will hold thee in talk till three of his ship-folk have crept between thee and the sea. Then he will draw weapon and fall upon thee—and we too with him; that was his mind; but we stand by thee, as thou knowest."

"Nay," said Olaf, "I thank you for your good service, but you shall have no hand in this slaying."

"Now, wilt thou not go back and take thy arms?"

But Olaf answered with flashing eyes, "God giveth angels; I walk not alone. Have no fear for me, and let us hasten."

Without a word the brothers bent to their oars, and the boat surged through the bright waters. As they landed and drew it up on the beach, Olaf picked two round stones from the shingle, and laid them in a fold of his cloak. At some little distance from the shore, Thori, who had heard the sound of the oars, came down to meet them.

Olaf strode rapidly in advance, and as the two men approached each other the traitor saw such a look of stormy splendour on the king's face that his false heart failed him. He stopped suddenly with a sharp cry: "I see it blazing in thine eyes. Thy kinsmen have betrayed me."

"Thou hast betrayed thyself," said Olaf; "and now sudden death lays hands on thee."

With outstretched arm Olaf leaped forward to seize the dastard, but Thori, stricken with panic, turned and fled.

"Thou canst not flee from thy terror," cried the king, "nor can swiftness save thee from me. Bring him down, Vigi; slay him if thou wilt."

The great dog gave tongue, and bounded in pursuit of the fugitive. At the same moment the brothers raised a warning shout, and Olaf turned to see the three shipmen running in upon him with uplifted axes.

He took the stones from his cloak, poised them one in each hand above his head, and measured the distance with glittering eyes. Then, deadly as lightning, both stones were hurled at once; there was a dull crash, and two of his assailants fell headlong to the earth. In a twinkling his cloak was flung off and grasped in readiness, but the third man held back white and trembling.

"Put thine axe in thy belt," said Olaf.

The shipman obeyed.

"See if thy comrades are dead."

"They are dead, king," the man replied; "thou hast shattered—"

"Enough! Go to Thori yonder, and see if he still lives."

"Call back thy hound, king."

The deep baying of the dog had ceased, and at Olaf's whistle Vigi raced back to his side.

"Thori is dead," said the seaman; "the hound has strangled him."

"Get to thy ship. Earl Hakon lies yonder in the fjord. If thou and thy fellows would go to him, you are free. If you will be my men, come to me to-morrow."

That night, in the darkness of a noisome hiding-place, Hakon was slain while he slept by his thrall Kark, and the traitor, who was born on the same day as the earl and had been given him in childhood, hastened to Ladir with his grey dishonoured head.

Early in the dazzle of the morning the six ships rowed, with war-horns sounding, up the fjord to Ladir. Hakon's men came down to meet them, but they were daunted by the array and wild clamour of the onset, and heading for the nearest shore, they took to the hills.

Joyously Olaf landed on the crowded wharf. The mere sight of the young hero—his lofty stature and singular beauty, his bright friendly look, blue eyes, and long yellow hair—drew the hearts of the people to him and they thronged about him with cries of welcome. Talk of his strength and prowess and of the strange events that had happened during the voyage passed from mouth to mouth, so that folk would hear of nothing but his being chosen king.

In the midst of this excitement came Kark the thrall with Hakon's head. He told Olaf of their flight and his slaying of his master. "And now, king," he said, "I saw in a dream how I was here in Ladir, and you put a costly jewel about my neck."

"That shall be a blood-red ring," said Olaf. "Give him the reward of the traitor."

The wood in the forest and the iron in the hills rejoiced as the axe sundered soul from body. The two heads were hung side by side for the choughs on the gallows-mound in the doom-ring of Nidarholm. Thither went the folk crying up to them with curses, and hurling stones. So bitter was the hatred in the land that for long afterwards men avoided Hakon's name and never spoke of him except as the Wicked Earl.

Then a "Thing" or great council of the people was summoned, and Olaf was chosen by the eight shires of Drontheim to rule over them. Straightway he spoke to them of the true God in the heavens, and of his wish that they should forsake sorcery and sacrifices and heathen worship and believe in Him alone. "For this have I come among you, that giving up the evil things of the olden time, you should accept baptism and come to the faith of Christ." He warned them that no man should henceforth seek to bring in whales or shoals of fish by magic songs, or sit out at midnight on the cross-roads to hold commerce with spirits of darkness. Then pointing to the temple hard by, which Earl Hakon had restored, "Ye know," he cried, "who gave you this temple. Ye have seen his head in the doom-ring; come and behold the gods in whom he trusted."

Breaking into the sacred enclosure, he and his sea-wolves hewed down the portals of the temple, and wrenched away the carved ring of massive gold with which Hakon had adorned it. With his own battle-axe Olaf dashed Thor from his high place, and the images of the other gods and goddesses were shattered to fragments. Then when the building had been despoiled of its rich hangings and its splendour of gold and silver, it was set on fire.

"Now you have seen with your own eyes," said the king, "what power these gods have to help themselves or any man. Wherefore I pray you heed my counsel, which is that you become Christ's men even as you are the king's."

When the winter drew to a close Olaf went out through the south country, imposing his kingship and declaring the true faith. Hakon's son, Earl Erik, had thought to make a stand with his kith and kin, but when he heard how the great lords and yeomen everywhere swore allegiance to the king, they escaped through the wild ways into Sweden. In the springtime Olaf reached Vikin, the old realm of his father Tryggva, and there he found, with great joy after so many years, his mother Astrid, and brothers and sisters, and many doughty men and fair women of his stock.

"Of all the folk in Norway," said he, "ye are dearest to me because of our blood. And, as is right, to you I look first for fellowship and help, for be sure of this that one of two things will happen, either that I make Norway a Christian land or lose my life."

"That last shall not happen to thee if we may hinder it," said Thorgeir, his half brother; "but we also look to thee, Olaf, for something, and that is favour and gentleness."

"Well you may," replied the king; "and who shall gainsay you? Powerful men I shall make you, if you will share in my labour. Fain, indeed, would I win all men by gentleness and peace to what is for their great good, both now and hereafter. But if there be stark and wayward fellows who would make head against the king, what choice is left for the king but to break them to his will? Have the folk of Norway forgotten how Hakon drove iron harrows over them in an evil cause? And shall I not be wrathful if they resist me when I would rid the land of wickedness and the rule of devils?"

So great was the love that went out to the high heart and brave presence of the king that everywhere in Vikin the images of the gods were overthrown and their temples destroyed. In many other places Bishop Sigurd went forth teaching and baptizing, though many consented through fear and against their liking. In Hordaland and Rogaland, however the yeomen were hardy and proud, and they prepared to stand by the dark worship of old days. When Olaf landed among them he invited the chief men to a feast, and after they had had much friendly talk together, he reproached them with the cruel blood-offerings which they made to Frey. They would neither deny their shame nor confess it.

"Then," said the king, "if you have been un- justly accused, it will be easy for you to obey me, and destroy Frey's image."

"That we shall never do. We have served him long, and well has he repaid us."

"Much I fear then that you are blood-guilty. Now listen to me. To-morrow we shall meet at the Thing. Frey shall be there. I shall question him and judge him. He shall make good his cause, else I will surely slay him, and teach you the good way which the High God has taught me."

In the grey of the morning, then, the king rowed to the great temple in the fjord. In the green meadows were Frey's stud horses; and Olaf, who had the horseman's word, called the sacred white stallion, which came whinnying to him. It was shod with silver, and its mane and tail were plaited with ribbons and gold thread. Olaf mounted it, and his men took the geldings, and they rode to the temple.

Alighting, Olaf went in and struck the idols down from their altars, but Frey he carried off unharmed to his ship. Long before the others he and his men got to the place of the Thing, and hid the image in his tent, and when the meeting had assembled he spoke to them for some time of the well-being of the land, the observance of good laws, and the duty of kings to have constant care for the peace and happy estate of their people.

"Enemies and evil-doers shall a true king bring to fair trial and sharp justice. What say you—shall a rich man or a mighty escape this law?"

"No, none," cried many voices in the crowd.

"No, none," rejoined the king, "not even though he be a god. Bring Frey to judgment; let him come freely if he will; if not, lay hands upon him."

So the king's men bore the great image from the tent, and placed it upright beside Olaf.

"Does any one know this respondent?"

"He is Frey, king, as thou knowest, our fathers' god and ours."

"How comes it you needs must worship him?"

"Very mighty we have thought him till now. Often aforetime has he spoken with us, and has given us fair seasons and plenty by sea and by land."

"Is he then less mighty now?"

"Not less mighty, but he is angered against us because of thee and the talk of thy God."

Olaf shook his head. "Never has he spoken to you, though it may be the Spirit of Darkness has spoken through his mouth. Witness now how I shall put him to fair trial."

Grasping his axe in his right hand, the king turned to the statue: "Frey, god of this people of mine speak now, if thou canst speak, some word in thy defence."

Frey was silent.

"Let the Evil then speak, which perchance is within thee, and which has long misled this people."

The Thing-folk held their breath to listen; in the stillness was heard the cry of the plover on the fell-side; but never a word came from Frey.

"If there be any strength or greatness in thee, Frey, or power to harm or spell to blight, use it now and spare not, for my hand is raised up against thee. If thou slumberest, awake; awake, for I am upon thee."

Olaf swung his axe aloft, but Frey did not move. He shore away his hand, but Frey heeded not. Then he smote him and clove him asunder.

"O you brave folk, whom I would have my friends, how shall I reason with you if your own eyes will not convince you? Hear, then, the choice I give you; receive the baptism of the living God, or do battle with me."

Happily the people submitted, and Olaf sailed away northward to the great council which had been called at Frosta. But the chiefs had sent out war-arrows, and the yeomen had come in arms—a great host who cried out in tumult against him when he spoke of change.

"When thou camest among us first," said Iron-beard of Yriar, "we thought it was heaven, and we rejoiced in thee as a man beloved of the gods; but thou hast deceived us. If it be still thy purpose to spoil us of our freedom, to burn our temples, and to send thy priest with the ram's-horn staff to wash us, we will drive thee out like Athelstan's foster-son."

Seeing that he could neither quell them nor persuade them at that time, the king answered graciously: "Truly, I would still have you think it heaven as when I came, and I would bind you to me in loyal fellowship. Thus far, therefore, I will make agreement with you. I will come to you again when you hold your great sacrifice, either at midsummer or at Yule-tide, and it may happen that my blood-offerings shall not be less than yours. Then we shall see together to be of one mind in the matter of our worship."

With this promise the people were well pleased, and Olaf returned to Vikin. Now at this time Sigrid the Haughty was Queen of Sweden, and she was a widow; and the thought came to Olaf that if he married her, all that great land of the north from sea to sea might be brought under the rule of Christ. The queen was not unwilling, and all went pleasantly with his suit until Olaf spoke of her christening.

"Oh, fair friend," said Sigrid, "in this I cannot yield to your wishes. You shall follow what faith you will, as indeed it becomes a king; but it would ill befit me who am queen of this realm to forsake lightly the worship of my fathers."

"Have you led me so far but to fool and flout me?" asked Olaf, rising hastily. "You knew well, I think, that I would wed no heathen woman." And as he spoke he shook his gloves in his vexation, and by ill chance the tips touched her cheek.

Then, too, Sigrid rose, with a dark flush on her face: "Little love, it appears, would have been lost between us; but this shame which you have done me may one day be your downfall."

So they parted suddenly in anger, and afterwards Olaf had cause to remember her words.

Now when the leaf was golden on the silver birch, Olaf spread sail again for the north, and when it was drawing towards Yule he invited the foremost men from all the country round to a feast. After they had made merry together, "You mind," he said, "how mad the folk were with me at the Frosta Thing and threatened to drive me out, and how we came to agreement. Now if the gods be as wroth with me as the folk were—and I will not deny the grievous despite I have done them—it will not be any small blood-offering that will appease them. They will look for as noble a sacrifice as king can make. No wretched thrall, robber, or broken man shall I dare to offer them, but it shall be men worthy of them, the noblest and best in the inlands and outlands. Here are their names."

Amid looks of dismay he read out a list of famous names, and at a sign from the king armed men stood with bare axes beside these chosen guests.

"These are the men I have honoured, and eager will they be to have the gods receive them and reward their faithful service."

"What," cried Olaf when loud murmurs rose from all sides of the hall, "do you misdoubt the power and goodness of the gods?" and making a long pause, he looked silently from face to face. "Why then will you not rather turn to Him who has made the heavens and the earth, who is as gracious as He is mighty, in whose thoughts there is no evil, and who will welcome you with no less love in your old age than when you are young?"

So the king got the better of these idolaters, and when the chief men had given hostages for their baptism he went up to Moere for the Yule sacrifice. Kolbiorn and Kiartan the Icelander and Halfred the Skald went with him, and they found a vast gathering of yeomen from the eight shires. Ironbeard their leader stood forth, and braved the king with loud words: "All we are of the same mind as we were at Frosta."

"What I promised at Frosta, that I hold to," replied Olaf. "I have come to enter into the temple with you."

In all the land of Norway there was no goodlier temple than this of Moere. The cross-beams were covered with plates of silver; the hangings were of sea-purple, and a gold chain was looped round the walls. There were many carved images of the gods, and Thor was in the midst, glittering with gold in a splendid chariot, and two he-goats were yoked to the chariot with a rope of twisted silver about their horns.

When Olaf had looked at Thor he raised his staff and struck him from his place. His companions flung down the other idols, and at the sound of their breaking, his men fell upon Ironbeard and slew him in the porch. Little gain had the yeomen from this Thing, for no one desired Olaf's blood-offerings, and the loss of their leader left them hopeless of victory. Wherefore they made their peace with the king.

Ironbeard was laid in his grave-mound, and a blood-fine for his slaying was awarded against the king's men, but Olaf offered as an atonement to take his daughter Gudrun for his queen. With great joy the dead man's kinsfolk came to their bridal, hoping for friendship and quiet days.

But that night, when all the palace lay in the stillness of sleep, Olaf awoke from a warning dream and saw Gudrun leaning over him. In her uplifted hand a dagger gleamed in the moonlight. She stood spell-bound before his calm gaze, and he arose, and taking the weapon from her, called her women. The moon had scarcely changed its place in heaven when the young queen and her company were riding to her home in Yriar. So bride and bridegroom parted without a word, never to meet again.

In this masterful fashion for the most part Olaf preached the Gospel to the rude and hardy race of a barbaric age. He bound the wizards to a reef at low-water, and the surf of the rising tide swept over the Skerry of Shrieks, and made an end of sorcery in Norway. Fugitives were run down like wolves. Rebels were burnt in their homesteads.

Raud the Strong was the last of the turbulent pagans who set him at defiance. When he heard that Olaf was bearing up to God's Isle in search of him, the fearless chief entered his temple, and called upon Thor: "Blow mightily in thy red beard, thou lord of the old land, and lift up thy storm-cry against this king!" The winds rose and came down in booming gusts from the hills. All that day the king's ships were stayed at the mouth of Salten Fjord; all that night they plunged and strained at their cables; and day broke in an angry glare of tempest.

Then Bishop Sigurd robed himself in white alb and gold-wrought cope, and raising aloft the cross, he set it on the prow of Olaf's ship. On either side he lit the sacred candles, and the flames burnt clear, with never a flicker in the still air; and still water lay about the bows. The rowers ran to their benches; the bishop intoned a hymn; the great ship felt the pull of forty oars, and as it sprang forward, a lane of glassy sea opened through the midst of the storm. But on either side, beyond the sweep of the oar-blades, the waves tossed up their white caps and the flying spindrift hid the shape of the hills.

Thus through the gales of Thor Olaf won to God's Isle, and Raud was surprised and taken. But though the sturdy pagan renounced his old creed—"Never again shall I bend to him who has betrayed me!"—he refused to believe in Christ, and died in torture.

THE LAST SEA-FIGHT

RUTHLESS as he was in spreading the true faith, no such king as Olaf had ever before been seen in Norway. The people loved him for his shining manliness. The most great-hearted, the blithest, the most impetuous of men was he; open-handed, and delighting in splendour. They forgave his violence for his justice, and his masterful spirit for his kindliness to the lowly.

Of his skill and strength his sea-wolves never tired of bragging; as swimmer, rock-climber, ski-man he had no rival. He could split an arrow with an arrow, and cast two spears at a time, right hand and left. Kiartan's ship he saved by main force when the cable parted; and when Eindridi saw him walk on the oars over the water while the rowers were rowing, and keep three daggers at play in the air, "Thine angels," he said, "help thee to do this, and I cannot contend against them."

Now when the king had slain Raud the Strong he brought away Raud's dragon-ship with him. Larger it was by far than the *Crane*; indeed there was no nobler ship in Norway, with the dragon's head and the coils of the tail overlaid with gold, and its sail which spread like a dragon's wing. Olaf himself steered it.

Sailing down by the steep coast, he saw a stranger standing upon a rock, and as the ship veered in so as well-nigh to graze it, the stranger climbed on board and saluted the king. He was young to look at, tall and handsome, red-bearded, and clad in green. He talked and laughed merrily with the seamen, and fell to wrestling with them, but the strongest there could not hold his own against him. Then he tolde them old-world tales of wonder. "In those times he said, "the folk of these fells and fjords were mighty friendly with me. In their need they called upon me for help, and I slew the giants for them. Friendly they would have been to this day had they not been mishandled in a way which may not altogether escape vengeance." Glancing sideways at Olaf, he uttered a jeering laugh and plunged overboard. Then the seamen knew that they had spoken face to face with Thor of the Thunder-hammer.

Not once or twice did trolls and creatures of darkness lurk in the forest or among the rocks of the shore to mock and fleer at the king, but their power of evil had passed from them. It was in these days that Hall and Thorhall the Seer were on the hillside, and as they sat silent Thorhall smiled. "Why are you smiling?" asked Hall. "I am smiling," said the Seer, "at the sight of so many of the doors of the hills wide open, and the little people bundling their wallets for a long wayfaring."

So well pleased was the king with Raud's dragon-ship that he laid the keel of another still larger and goodlier, and his own he called the *Long Serpent* and Raud's the *Short*. He was yet busied with this work when a sail put in to Ladir, and it bore Thyra, the sister of Sweyn the Forked-beard. Sorely against her will Sweyn had given her to Burislaf, the old heathen King of Wendland; but with him she would not stay, neither would she eat or drink, and at last, under cloud of night, she fled through the wilds with her foster-father, and took ship to Olaf for refuge and counsel. She was fair and young, and of the king's faith, and he saw not how he might mend her fortunes so well as by sharing his throne with her.

Now it was not long after their marriage that Thyra began to fret over the fair estates which she owned in Wendland, and urged Olaf to claim their revenues for her. "So good a friend of thine is Burislaf that he will readily grant whatever thou may'st ask, and these lands I hold in my own right." "Hast thou not all thou canst desire?" asked Olaf. "Why should such thoughts trouble thee?"

Still she repined, and often during that winter she was in tears over her grievance. The king spoke of the matter with his secret counsellors, but they besought him to wait for change and chance, and not to waste the lives of tall men by stirring in so doubtful a cause. In the early spring it chanced upon the Sunday of Palms that Olaf saw a man with fragrant sprays of angelica, and gaily carried some to Thyra. She was in a petulant mood, and put them from her with graceless words:

"It is easy to see that I am but a beggarly queen when thou thinkest angelica leaves should please me. A pity Sweyn should so daunt thee that I may not enjoy what is my own!"

Olaf flushed red with anger: "God's splendour, what an asp may lurk in a rosy mouth! Better all thy revenues were at the bottom of the deep sea than the bones of but a score of my ship-folk. But no man shall ever say that thy brother Sweyn could make me go in fear of him."

Then, as the rhymes of the old song go,

> "Wilful as wind,
> Neither to hold nor bind,"

he left her, and she was sorry enough that she had angered him. He had the *Long Serpent* finished and launched from the slips, and that summer he manned her as never war-ship had been manned in those seas. Red Wulf guarded the king's banner at the prow, and in that peerless company were Kolbiorn, called King's Shadow, because he was so like the king, Thorstein the White, Hyrning and Thorgeir, Olaf's half-brothers, and heroes as many more than can be named. No man among them had more than sixty or less than twenty years to his age except Einar the Archer. He was in his eighteenth summer, but he drew the strongest bow and shot the surest arrow in Norway.

Southward with a great host of sail they fared for Wendland, and in one place and another along the coast the king landed to cheer and strengthen the folk in their new faith. Strange things happened in those glowing summer nights, for while deep slumber lay on the ships and guards kept watch on shore, the king would suddenly come upon them from inland when they thought him sleeping. No one had seen him go ashore; none knew whence he came; there was no trace of footsteps on sand or dewy grass.

All this greatly troubled Thorkel, who wondered whether indeed the king went thus abroad in the dead night season, or if it were some spirit of evil which assumed the king's likeness. Wherefore, upon a night when he knew that Olaf was on board, he set himself to watch at the foot of the gangway between ship and shore. Slowly passed the hours of the dreamy twilight; the breeze of the morning began to blow cold, and Thorkel had just thought, "This night at least he has slept sound," when iron arms were cast about him, and he was flung into the sea.

"That for meddling!"

At the sound of the king's voice Thorkel feared he was angry, but Olaf threw him a rope, and laughed as he hauled him on board.

"I did not mean to vex thee," said Thorkel.

"Thou, of all men, art never like to vex me," replied Olaf, and indeed the man was his bosom-friend and counsellor; "but when I saw thee standing there, I could not keep my hands from making sport of thee."

"Thou hast made sport of my cloak," said Thorkel. "Let not that grieve thee to the soul; thou shalt have another cloak."

"And if thy enemies, men or devils, lie in wait for thee, and fall upon thee and spoil *thee*, wilt thou give us another Olaf?" asked Thorkel. "What folly is this in a great chief, to wander far away from his ships, unarmed and alone!"

"Dear man, have no care for me," replied the king; "no evil can befall me whither I go."

On the following night the king touched Thorkel's feet to awake him, and signed to him to dress; and they went ashore together, and passed near the watchers, but these paid no heed to them.

"Dost thou see?" asked Olaf. "While my arm is in thine, no one is aware of thee or me. Now, if thou wilt, thou shalt fare with me whither I fare, but thou shalt swear never to speak of this night's doings so long as I am king."

Inland they went till they came to a pine-wood, and in the clearing of the trees there stood a fair house.

"Abide here till I return," said Olaf; and he entered, but did not quite close the door; and Thorkel saw that the house was dazzling with light, and filled with a fragrance which took away all feeling of care or sorrow, or of weight or weariness. In the midst knelt the king with his arms raised to heaven; and out of the great light came stately and gracious beings in white robes, and they blessed the king and raised him to his feet. Then out of the fragrance came a throng of little children singing, and they too were in white raiment bordered with gold, and rosebuds and green leaves were woven in their bright hair.

Then Olaf came forth, and the house fell into darkness within; but the king brought with him an after-glow of the light and a lingering of the fragrance. And as they returned through the pine-wood Thorkel looked back, but the fair house had vanished from the clearing.

One other thing there is to tell of this sea-faring. While they lay off Hildsholm one of the shipmen made a wager to climb the great rock,

176

Smalsar Horn. A perilous place it is beyond most, springing high and sheer out of the sea, and its sharp spit of stone stands solitary in the heavens. When this man had gone far up, he came to such a pass that he could neither ascend higher nor yet get down again. Then the king, laughing with a lad's glee, slung his shield over his shoulders, and went up the rock, calling to the man, "Bide there till I come." Right to the top of the Horn he won, and fastened his shield to the spit, so that it glittered like a star. As he made it fast, his dream of the stone pillar in Garda rose up in his mind; and for a moment he seemed to behold around him once more fields of summer flowers and the fair white company of happy souls. And he wondered within himself, "Is this a sign? Yet shall it give me neither fear nor misgiving." And descending swift and light-hearted, he took the shipman under his mighty arm, and brought him down to a safe place.

Along the Danish shores and down through Eyra Sound they fared without hindrance, and came at length to Wendland, where with great friendliness King Burislaf gave them welcome. He was the father of Geira whom Olaf first loved; and when they came to speak of Thyra's claims the old king readily granted all that was right and seemly, and that trouble was brought to a happy close.

So Olaf tarried long in Wendland, forgathering with old friends, and the time fleeted by in revelry and good-fellowship. Most of all he was glad at heart to meet once more with Astrid, Geira's young sister, who was now the wife of Sigvald, Earl of the Jomsvikings. Yet, could he have foreseen it, this joy and remembrance of early love were but the last bright threads running through the dark with which the picture of his life was being woven.

Now before these things had happened, when the first rumour of the king's sailing reached Denmark, Sigrid the Haughty was queen of that land, for she had married Sweyn Forked-beard; and she cast about in her subtle mind how she might turn this venture to Olaf's undoing. She had never forgiven him, and when she thought of the slight he had put upon her, the flick of his glove seemed still burning on her cheek. She let slip no chance of stirring up strife between

Sweyn and his old Viking comrade, and when all other means failed she burst into angry tears:

"Woe's the day I listened to a king who dare not avenge my wrongs! Yet, poor man, why should I upbraid thee with my shame, when thou canst not avenge thy own? When Olaf took thy sister Thyra, was it with leave asked of thee? And now, they say, he is to raid Wendland for revenues that by right are no longer hers. Had thy father, old Harald Blue-tooth, been alive, would he have put up meekly with these affronts?"

She so fretted and stung him with her taunts that he too flared out in wrath: "True it is also I might to-day have been King in England had he not broken faith and made peace with Ethelred."

Then Queen Sigrid spun out webs of craft to close about Olaf and bring him to his death in the Baltic sea-ways.

"Alone," she said, "thou canst not cope with him on water, but the Jomsvikings will join thee; my son shall aid thee with the power of Sweden; and who but Earl Erik will be keen of this chance to lay hold on Norway, and pay Olaf back for his father's head on the gallows-tree? To Wendland Olaf shall fare with a proud heart; what his home-coming shall be lies in thy hand."

So kings and earls were leagued together, but Sigvald, the leader of the Jomsvikings, would have no hand in the plot, except that he consented to keep Olaf in Wendland long enough for the hostile fleets to gather. Out of Sweden and Denmark they came in vast numbers, and masking themselves with green boughs they lay under Hiddensee on the Svold, which is the Race of the sea near Rugen Isle.

For all their care the plotters could not keep their secret, and rumours spread to Wendland of a mighty thronging of ships in the western narrows, and many surmised that this could mean no less than war. Already the Northmen were wishing for home, and they pressed the king to return. "Free you are to go at any time," replied Olaf, "but I shall think those most friendly who tarry for me." None would leave him, and, disquieted and impatient, the Northmen waited until it was his pleasure to depart.

On the eve of their sailing, Astrid came at night to warn him of his danger, and to join forces with him if he would accept her aid; but Olaf answered cheerily: "More ways than one I see out of this peril, little sister, but never shall I shrink from the challenge of my foes. And why should I embroil thee with thy neighbours, dear heart? Nay, the issue is in God's hands, all-powerful to keep my kingdom mine or to give it to another."

"Yet I shall sail with thee," said Astrid. "Do but throw back thy head for a sign, and thou shalt have what service I can do thee."

As the king held her hand at parting, "Dost thou mind, little sister," he asked, "how long ago we sat in hall and Gizur made songs of the folk in the tapestry?"

"I mind it well," said Astrid, leaning closer to him. "Ay, and Geira said, how these folk, once happy and glad to be alive, were all now dead and half forgotten, and served but to keep out the cold wind?" Astrid inclined her head silently.

"So perchance it may be with us, and minstrels by the winter fire may make songs of our images. But we knew not then that the end of all was otherwise. Hence we shall fare when our earthly day is done; but in the high halls of the Lord God we shall be, not as dead folk in pictures, but living men and women still. Sleep light of heart, sister; He that keeps us will not slumber."

Early on the morrow "All aboard!" was sounded, and hawsers were cast loose, and all put out to sea—sixty of the king's ships and eleven under Sigvald. Westward they bore, the small sail drawing away in the light wind, and the great warships moving more slowly. And ever there was a Wendish *skeid*—nearer at one time and further off at another—which hung within hail of the *Long Serpent*.

Under Hidden's Island lay Sweyn and the Swede king and Earl Erik, and at the first glimmer of the coming sails they went up with numbers of their men to the wooded hill, and watched the small ships of the Northmen go to the open sea. Fair was the wind, and brightly the September sun shone over the Svold, and when the larger ships drove in from the offing, first one and then another was taken for the king's great dragon. Again and yet again men cried out in wonder, "Here it comes!" but Erik laughed, "Many more splendid ships has King Olaf than these; let them go!" So, sail after sail, more than half of the great fleet swept through the narrows, and no one suspected the foe lying in ambush.

Then out of the east came the cruisers of the Jomsvikings, and with them three stately vessels. One of these was the *Crane* and another the *Short Serpent* of Raud. And Sweyn cried out joyfully, "Aboard, aboard! High shall the *Long Serpent* carry me before sunset, and this hand shall wind her larboard and starboard at my will."

"Even this ship," rejoined Earl Erik testily, "thou couldst scarce wrest from him with thy Danes alone; but King Olaf has a better."

And as they went down from the hill they saw yet a fourth great vessel. Its prow was a grim dragon's head blazing in gold over the sea, and its strong sides were in their height and their length such an amazement that silence and fear fell upon the enemy as they got to their ships.

Thus far had all gone prosperously with the Northmen, and there was no sign of Queen Sigrid's guile; but as these large ships entered the Svold the Jomsvikings suddenly dropped sail and rowed closer in to the island.

"Here will I await King Olaf," said Sigvald. "It seems to me there is a great crowd of folk on the island and that peril lies ahead."

The captains of the *Crane* and the *Short Serpent*, astonished by this strange shift and uncertain what it might mean, lowered their sails also. So did the other ships, and all lay-to for Olaf to come up to them. But scarcely had the *Great Dragon* stood in to windward when the leagued fleets shot out from their ambush and swarmed over the Race.

"Bear on, king," Thorkel cried to Olaf; "drive out to the open sea; the odds here are too heavy for thee."

"Strike sails! Out oars!" Olaf answered with a ringing cry. "Let no man here think of flight. God look to my life, I shall fight blithely in this place. Lash ships together!"

The war-horns sounded the signals, and the Norse ships gathered about the *Great Dragon*—the *Crane* to weatherward, the *Short Serpent* to lee, and the rest four deep on either side. Eleven ships in all, and they were lashed gunwale to gunwale. So vast was the length of the *Long Serpent* that her forecastle lay out alone far forward of the others.

"If we lie in this way," said Red Wulf, "we shall have wild weather behind these bulwarks."

"Ay?" said Olaf. "It was ever my intent that the *Dragon* should be in the forefront; I thought not to have a craven to ward my banner."

Red Wulf flung back a scornful gibe, and Olaf, snatching his bow, set an arrow to the string.

"Shoot at thy foes, king. Belike thou wilt not have too many men by the sun goes down."

Then came the Wendish *skeid* under the *Dragon's* quarter, and a man at the prow spoke to the king in a strange tongue, and Olaf answered him cheerily. "This is one of our Wendish friends," he said, as the *skeid* passed astern, and rowing near to the shore came to anchor. Afterwards it was in the minds of many that the Lady Astrid might have been on board that ship.

From the poop of the *Dragon* Olaf looked out over the sea, and as he beheld the throng of his foes, he thought with a twinge of regret of the many goodly ships that had fared out to the open sea. Yet his words were gay and proud-hearted. "That banner over against us is King Sweyn's," he said with a laugh. "Danes do not beat Northmen. Leave them out of the reckoning. Who is yonder?"

"Thy namesake, Olaf the Swede."

"Home were a better place for the Lap-King! And those tall ships to windward?"

"That is Earl Erik Hakonson."

"Northmen like ourselves. The earl will look to us for a battle of giants to-day."

Then the horns sounded onset, and with the hoarse whoop of war sixty Danish ships swooped down on the *Great Dragon* in a storm of arrows. The Northmen grappled them with hooks, and shot down upon them from their high decks; and all they grappled they cleared of men and cast adrift. King Sweyn fell back in confusion, and the Lap-King fell upon the *Dragon* with fifteen ships. They too were grappled with steel, and the decks reddened with slaughter.

Meanwhile, on the flank of the fierce fighting, came Erik in *Ironbeard*, which bristled with spikes from prow to sea, and attacked the outer ships. Many fell upon both sides, but Olaf's men were driven inward from vessel to vessel, and as each was cleared the lashings were sundered and the next was boarded. Danes and Swedes thronged about *Ironbeard* and made good Erik's losses, but every Northman that fell left Olaf the weaker. At last all the king's ships were ravaged and cut adrift, and on the decks of the *Great Dragon* were crowded all the fighting men of Norway.

All that day the youngest of them, Einar the Archer, had plied his bow doughtily, and twice had Erik felt the wind of his arrows.

"Shoot me that tall young man," cried the earl to Finn of Herland.

"That man bears a charmed life to-day, lord," replied Finn, "yet I may mar his shooting."

Now Finn had fashioned Einar's bow, and as Einar bent it against the earl for the third time, Finn sent a bolt which snapped it in his grasp.

"What was it that broke?" asked Olaf as he heard the sound.

"Norway from thy hand, king," said Einar.

"More noise would have come of so great a breaking," replied Olaf. "Norway does not hang on thy bow. Take mine!"

Einar took it and drew the horns till the length of the arrow came short of the stretch. "Too weak a bow for so mighty a king!" he said, and throwing it aside he caught up his shield and joined the slayers.

Once did the earl board the *Long Serpent*, but the king's men stoutly drove him back. "A bold feat!" exclaimed Olaf; "but the earl, I think, will not clear the *Dragon* while Thor is his shipmate" —for on prow of *Ironbeard* dwelt a golden idol of Thor.

After that Erik put in to land with his wounded and slain, and he bade Danes and Swedes pluck up courage and make another onset, if they would not be shamefully vanquished by a single ship. Then once again the Wendish *skeid* came out to Olaf: "Our men will fight for you, will gladly die or win with you, whichever way fortune goes." But the king would not take their help. "Yet you may be of good service to me," he said, "if you will stay upon the spot where you have been all day."

So the *skeid* returned to anchor; and *Ironbeard* came again to the attack, and all about Dane and Swede darted and stung like a host of hornets. Great logs were hoisted and dropped on board the *Dragon* till she took a heavy list to weatherward, and Erik's men swarmed over the bulwarks.

Thrice did Olaf hurl his spears, double-handed, at the earl, but Erik stood unscathed. "Little wonder!" said Olaf when he perceived that the dweller of the prow had been changed, and in the place of Thor a gold cross stood on *Ironbeard*.

The forecastle was abandoned, and the Northmen, drunk with the joy of battle, slowly yielded foot by foot as they drew aft. In that last heroic stand were Hyrning and Thorgeir, Red Wulf and Einar, and Kolbiorn King's Shadow, who had dressed so like the king as to fill men's minds with uncertainty which was which.

High on the poop stood Olaf in gilded helm, with his shield glittering on his arm, and over his sark of ring-mail he wore a sleeveless coat of scarlet silk. When Kolbiorn went up and stood beside him, it seemed as though there were two kings.

As the earl's horde made a fierce rush a blaze of splendour came from the setting sun, so that the figures on the poop seemed to vanish in its brightness. And when that wondrous light abated there was no one seen in Olaf's place, and the last of the stalwart men of the *Great Dragon* plunged into the sea.

A frantic clamour of victory rose from the allied fleets. In the swarms of skiffs and cutters chasing the Northmen who had gone overboard the seamen joined in the exultant cry, and ceased from slaying. Treacherous friends and craven foes, the Jomsvikings rowed cheering into the tossing field of conflict.

In the midst of the wild commotion, the oars of the Wendish *skeid* flashed through the water, and racing eastward for home, that gallant little ship disappeared in the shades of the twilight.

Of the last defenders of the *Dragon*, Kolbiorn and Einar the Archer and Thorkel were saved; and Earl Erik steered the peerless ship to Vikin, and they sailed with him. When they had moored to the quay,

Einar spoke to Vigi, who had lain on the poop all through the fight: "All is over now, Vigi, and we are masterless men."

THE NORTHMEN . . . SLOWLY YIELDED FOOT BY FOOT.

Springing to his feet, the great dog flung up his head, howling with anguish, and followed Einar ashore. Hard by the haven was a green howe looking over the sea, and Vigi ran to the top of it, and laid him low with tears running down his face. Kindly folk brought him food, but never again did he eat or drink; and there they found him dead.

So, in the splendour of the setting sun, the armed figure of the king vanished from Norway. For many a winter the people talked of the swift Wendish *skeid* rowing hard into the shadows of the September twilight, and foretold that Olaf would surely come again. The wild swans sang in the summer night; angelica stalks were fragrant in the early spring; but never more was the king seen in Norway.

The folk lamented him, and they most who knew him best, and long afterwards was remembered the song which Halfred the Skald made of him.

> "All over Norway, when Olaf was here,
> The high cliffs seemed laughing; but ever since then
> The sea-ways are joyless, the hillsides are drear,
> And restless I roam, the forlornest of men."

THE JORSALA PILGRIMS

IT was many a winter after the Svold sea-fight; and Gaut and Runolf were pilgrims from Iceland in Jorsala Land. They had drunk of the well at Nazareth. They had seen the snows of Hermon. By the sea of Galilee they had sat among the flowering grasses, the pink flax and the tall daisies growing over the carved stones of Capernaum. They had bathed in the sacred waters of Jordan.

In the Holy City of Jorsala they had prayed at the tomb wherein the body of the Lord was laid, and had bowed down before the wood of the cross on which He died. Upon the spot on which the Temple of King Solomon had stood there stood now a glittering dome with curtains of brocade, and within it they beheld the rock which is the oldest rock in all the world. Thereon in ancient summers did the threshers winnow the sheaves of Araunah. Beneath that rock there is a cave; and ever on the night before Easter morn may be heard the hollow voices of all the patriarchs and prophets of Israel giving thanks to God for the resurrection of the Lord. In that cave they say there is a well, which is called the Well of the Leaf, for one who went down into it found a path which led to the gates of Paradise, and he brought back a leaf plucked from the Tree of Weird, on which the destinies of men are written.

When they had seen Bethlehem—'tis a little white town on a hill, and below it lie the starry fields of the Shepherds—they desired to gaze upon the way by which Moses had led the children of Israel out of the House of Bondage, and they faced towards Gaza. Resting at fall of night by their tent fire, Gaut asked:

"Have the things on which we have looked brought thee nearer to the Lord?"

"That I scarce know," said Runolf. "It was great joy and expectation to come hither. Far have we travelled and fared hard, and perchance it should content us that we have often thought of Him. But never has it happened that a third has joined us two by the way, and that we felt our hearts burn within us while He spoke. When day has been far spent strangers have broken bread with us, but never have our eyes been opened to know Him by our fire. I had in some manner hoped that somewhere we might have felt that He was close to us. We have gone the ways He went, but if we ever touched the ground touched by His feet there was no sign to tell us of it."

"Nowhere have I seen Him," said Gaut, "not even in sleep."

"He is no longer living in this land," continued Runolf. "The wind has blown abroad the dust in which He wrote. The rain has washed the rock on which He trod. We have been looking for the shadows of a dream. Less easy has it been to feel Him beside me on the mountain or the shore than it is now to make-believe we two are now sitting on Blue Shaw Heath."

Then, after a pause, he added: "Blue Shaw Heath! Dost thou mind the ruddy moorland and the great bow of blue glacier? No fairer spot on a summer night have I seen on earth. I shall never see it again!"

"There are many weathers in a week," said Gaut, "and more in a month. What ails thee to-night?"

"I know not; such foreboding as might trouble a woman."

From Gaza, the city of sweet wells and green garths, they took the route which goes through the Desert to the Red Sea; but as the day began to decline a sudden sickness fell upon Runolf, and he could go no further. He was laid in the shadow of a tent, and Gaut sat with the sick man's head upon his knees. The Arabs came and looked at him. They saw that his face was drawn, and in his eyes was no intent to live, and one of them bethought him of the convent of holy men on the edge of the Desert, where there is ever some *hakeem* skilled in the virtues of herbs and balsams. They gathered about Gaut speaking eagerly all together and gesticulating towards the north-east, but he could not understand them. Then two of them mounted their horses and galloped over the shifting sands, where no man's footsteps abide.

The sun went down, and Runolf lay still, scarcely speaking at all, save to murmur his thanks when his comrade moistened his lips with wine. As the darkness fell, the Arabs kindled a fire, and little flames glimmered out far away in the Desert where the nomads had pitched their tents. Flashes of summer lightning began to play along the horizon, and some of these grew so large and dazzling that it seemed as if the heavens were opening.

All at once Runolf sat up, and grasping Gaut's hand, he pointed before him: "Look, look! Didst thou see Him? He is near us. There!"

For an instant, leagues of the Desert sprang out in the vivid flash, but Gaut saw nothing except sand and stones.

"He is close to us. I was wrong. He still lives in this land," said Runolf.

Then as yet another blaze of light expanded, "He has vanished from our sight," said Runolf; "but I have seen Him, as Peter saw Him, and John and Lazarus." And he sank back and lay in a glad stillness.

Out of the Desert came the Arab horsemen and a company of monks from the convent. They laid Runolf on a litter, and Gaut walked by his side as they bore him towards little specks of fire far away in the vast trackless night. Beyond these lights there were others; and yet again they guided their steps till they came to a rocky strath, with running water and palm-trees and olives. Here in the darkness it seemed as though they had entered into a maze of living stars, but these were fire-flies swarming among the rocks and trees.

In the cloister of the convent they were met by a man of mighty stature, aged and handsome. He bowed to Gaut with a kindly look and then leaned over his companion. He touched the sick man's face and closed his open eyes; and turning to Gaut, he asked in a gentle voice—

"You are Northmen?"

"Ay, lord; from Iceland. This is Runolf Grimason of Sheepfell by Blue Shaw Heath. My name is Gaut Ormson of Haukness."

"You have come far," said the tall man; "and to-night thy friend has fared further. No more can we help him, nor has he need we should. Be not too sorrowful for this. But now thou shalt rest and sleep, as is the privilege of sorrow. These shall watch beside thy friend, and to-morrow I will speak with thee."

On the morrow Gaut looked for the last time on Runolf, and the dead man's face seemed to have grown younger, and there was no line of disquietude in it. The brethren put a palm-branch between the dead pilgrim's hands, and laid him to rest in a tomb cut out of the rock on the strath side.

Then the kingly old man took Gaut's arm, saying, "Come now, brother, if it please thee to converse with me." He seemed to be the abbot of that house, for wheresoever he came monks and priests rose and stood ready to do him service; and he held himself so high above others that Gaut, who was no small man, scarce reached the masses of silvery hair which hung about his shoulders. He led Gaut to a fair stone house set among the palm-trees in the strath and laid fruit and bread and wine before him.

"Tell me first," he said, "whither thou wouldst go; or would it please thee to abide here and become one of us."

"Nay, I thank you, lord, but I will home again, and die among my neighbours."

"No need at all to die," replied the abbot cheerfully, "but if it be in thy mind to return home, I will give thee, when thou wilt, such furtherance as I may command."

Then having questioned him of his pilgrimage and of the men and places he had seen, "Now," said he, "good man from Iceland, tell me some news of thy home folk. Is Halfred the Skald still alive—him they called the Troublesome Poet?"

"King Olaf gave him that name," said Gaut. "He is dead, lord, these many winters. When the king fell in the Svold fight such anguish came upon him that he had no peace anywhere, but wandered restlessly as thistle-down in the wind. This, indeed, he said in one of his songs."

"Dost thou remember it, brother?"
"It ran thus," replied Gaut.
"'All over Norway, when Olaf was here,
The high cliffs seemed laughing; but ever since then
The sea-ways are joyless, the hillsides are drear,
The wild flowers are withered, the green tree is sere,
And I whirl like a leaf, the most restless of men.'

This, too, if one might repeat it, is another song he made:

"'When the battle-horns blared in the shock of the ships,
Would that I had been there, with a song on my lips!
Though but little the luck that a lone hand could bring,
It were heaven to have struck by the side of the king.
There is nought to replace, day or night, to the end,
In my thought the king's face, in my sight the true friend!'

A great song he made upon the Creation of the World, and that was in atonement of the transgressions of his youth when yet he worshipped the heathen spirits. He died in a wild storm on a voyage to Greenland, for a great wave dashed the boom upon him, and that killed him. His last words were a song, though I do not remember it aright. 'There is a lady,' he said, 'who will weep for me though of old I was her sorrow; yet freely would I now die, did I know that God would receive my soul.' They laid him in an oaken chest with an arm-ring of gold, a helmet, and a rich cloak. These were gifts he had of King Olaf. When they gave him to the sea, winds and waters bore him far, and the chest came ashore on the holy island of Iona; but thralls broke it open, and stealing the precious things, they cast the body into a marsh. 'Tis said that King Olaf appeared to the abbot in a vision. That I know not, but the guile of the thralls was discovered. Halfred was laid with honour in the church; of the arm-ring was made a chalice, of the cloak a cloth for the altar, and candlesticks of the helmet."

"It is strange to think of," said the abbot pacing to and fro. "And what of Kiartan?"

"He too is dead," said Gaut. "Ever he was seen to be a man fore-doomed. Folk say he loved the king's sister Ingebiorg, and when they kissed at parting 'twas a sore farewell. But Gudrun, who loved him above all the men in Iceland, brought him to his death. Bolli, his best friend, slew him, and yet loved him so that he held him in his arms till he died. The church at Burg, whither his body was borne, had been newly blest and was still hung in white. And this was a kindly chance in a hard weird, for Kiartan was the first man who kept Lent in Iceland, fasting and faring meagrely on the fruits of the earth."

"He was a goodly man," said the abbot, "and the king's sister did not need to love a nobler. But answer me this now. Is any memory of King Olaf kept green among you northern folk?"

"Ay, lord," said Gaut. "Glorious is the memory of that king, for he brought the realm to the creed of Christ."

"And what do folk say in these days of the sea-fight at Svold? I have heard that the king did not perish in that fight, but lived long after—even to the days of the kings who now rule."

"THESE, WHEN THOU GOEST," HE SAID, "I PRAY THEE TAKE TO EINAR."

"Many are the voices, and one says, and the other gainsays. Folk think that the king sank in his mail and made an end. Folk think that at the moment of the great light God took him. Folk think, too, that the king dived and swam beneath the great ships, and was carried away into safety by his Wendish friends."

"That last were more likely to happen," said the abbot, "than that he should have been caught up into Paradise. Some good, perchance, he did in his life, but he was a sinful man—even as I. Now tell me, what hast thou heard of Einar Tamberskelver? Does he still live?"

"Yea, and a mighty lord he is, and well loved."

"Greater archer than he there was not in Norway when he was young; and no man on the *Dragon* did more valiant deeds;" and the abbot, rising from his seat, brought from a chest a kingly belt and dagger. "These, when thou goest," he said, "I pray thee take to Einar, and greet him for me with this message, that he said a true word when he spoke of the breaking of the great bow of Norway from the king's hand."

"Very willingly," replied Gaut; and as he paused as if in doubt of something, the abbot asked him, "What is in thy thought?"

"I had a thing to say, if I might say it."

"Speak freely," said the abbot.

"Once when I was a lad I saw King Olaf. It is long ago; but changing gold for silver and the bloom of youth for the majesty of age, you, lord, remember me strangely of him. I pray you tell me whether you are not indeed King Olaf?"

"I knew the man, brother," answered the abbot, "and no one stood nearer to him than I in the last sea-fight; but I bear not his name, and I desire not his glory."

Some days thereafter, when Gaut had rested, the abbot provided him with all he needed, and gave him guides, who led him through the hills and the old Forest of Assur till he came to the sea and there found a ship for Greenland. All things were done in obedience to the abbot's word, as though he were a king in that land.

When Einar received his gift and heard his message his eyes filled with tears. "I would I had been with thee, Gaut," he said, "for this was no other than King Olaf that spoke with thee."

Now, when Edward the Confessor was king, it was his custom to read to his great men from the saga of King Olaf at Eastertide; "for," said he, "as Easter day is the greatest and most glorious of all days, so was this king the best and most illustrious of all the kings of our age." This he did ever as the feast of the Lord arisen came round.

One Easter Sunday when they had heard how the king escaped from the sea and had reached Jorsala Land, and there withdrawn to the peace of the cloister, King Edward closed the book and stood up beside the throne.

"To what we have read this day, I add this word," he said. "Pilgrims, returning from the holy places, have brought tidings of what we knew not until now. King Olaf whom we loved is dead. Pray for his soul. *Suscipiat te, rex meus, Christus qui te vocavit*—May Christ who called thee receive thee, my king!"

"I SAW THREE SHIPS A-SAILING"

A GUN was fired at sunset. It was the signal for the vesper hymn, and for the shifting of the course of the three caravels to due west. The lateen sails, long and shapely as a swallow's wings, were hauled closer to the wind, and the *Ace*, which was the fastest sailer of the three, stood down a way of billowy fire which ran straight into the blazing orb of the sun. Then with a strange and thrilling sound in the infinite spaces of those silent seas rose the strains of the *Salve Regina*, the mariner's evening prayer:

> "Hail, Queen! Mother of compassion,
> Life, sweetness, and hope of us, hail!"

The crew were still singing when the sun dipped. The track of fire died out along the heaving waters. For a few moments longer the small clouds of the trades shone in gold and rose-colour; then the warm hues faded, and the wondrous lights of heaven powdered the blue-green of the night.

The illimitable ocean, which had all day long been of deep blue, turned to a pale spectral luminousness. The long billows curled and broke in lines of flying sapphire. Gushes of liquid flame washed the sides of the caravel. Medusæ floated past in tangles and sprays of jewels. Trails of green light showed the web of death woven by the sharks as they crossed and re-crossed each other. Far astern, the shimmering wake of the *Ace* seemed to mark out the path for the *Lassie* and the *Blessed Mary*, on whose canvas the green crosses and the 'scutcheon of Castile were no longer visible, but lanterns burned at the mast-heads and high upon the castled poops.

On board the *Ace* the seamen stood together forward in small groups with their faces turned westward. Tried men they were, young for the most part and all but three of them Spaniards. That night there would be no sleep for any, unless it were for the sick. They were nearing the goal of their adventure. At any moment the dim summits of the Land of Gold and Spices might eclipse the clear stars which blazed low down on the horizon. At latest it would surely appear in the white glimmer of the dawn, and silk doublet and king's pension would fall to the lucky mortal who first sighted it.

In those steady winds, the course once set, there was seldom need to touch a sail from watch to watch, Over the long swells, teeming and sparkling with life, the small caravel of fifty tons kept her lead, but monotony, inaction, and fatigue began to have their effect on the men in spite of their keen expectancy on this last of the nights, of which there had been so many. Drowsiness was creeping over them when suddenly the thrumming of a guitar arose, and *Oye!* and *Brava!* from a dozen voices welcomed the player. "A *cantilena*, Pedro, a *madrigal*, a *balada*, anything to clear the dust out of our eyes."

"*Caballeros*," replied Pedro, "I give you the very honourable and melancholy ditty of San Pedro de Cardeña," and clearing his throat while he twanged a brisk prelude, the seaman sang:

"In San Pedro de Cardeña,
High in his ivory chair,
With face so fresh and comely,
With eyes so bright and fair,
With vast white beard in order,
For six long years and more
Had sat the great dead hero,
The Cid Campéador.

"All richly carved and golden
Rose o'er the ivory seat
The blazoned baldachino;
But at the dead Cid's feet
The beautiful Xiména,
The wife he loved so dear,
Lay wrapped in silk and spices
Within her sepulchre.
A Child's Book of Warriors
"Clad in his crimson mantle,
He sat erect and grand.
The long strings of his mantle
He held in his right hand;
His mighty sword Tizona,
Which many a Moor had cleft,
Sheathed in its graven scabbard,
Was lying on his left.

"In San Pedro de Cardéna
Each year they sanctified
With solemn mass and sermon
The day the great Cid died.
The monks sang Miserere,
The abbey bells were tolled,
The poor were fed at table
And clothed against the cold.

"Upon the seventh high feast-day,
Behold, it came to pass
There thronged a countless gathering
To hear the dead Cid's mass;
For Jew and turbaned Moslem
Had swarmed from near and far—
Foul dogs!—to gaze upon thee,
My hero of Bivar.

"And when the mitred Abbot,
Don Garci, saw how great

The crowd in the cathedral,
The crowd about the gate,
He came down from the pulpit;
'My sons, go forth,' said he,
'And I will preach my sermon
Beneath the walnut-tree.'
"Now, while he there stood preaching,
Within the chapel hid,
A Jew, a miscreant, lingered
Before the stately Cid,
Marvelling to see him seated
Upon his ivory chair,
With beard so long and hoary,
And face so fresh and fair,

"And holding in his right hand
His cloak-strings, while the brand—
The mighty sword Tizona
Lay sheathed in his left hand.
And when this unbeliever
Turned from the ivory throne
And peered about the chapel,
He saw that he was alone!

"Now loud and clear, now fainter,
The Abbot's speech he heard;
He heard the great tree's branches
By fitful breezes stirred;
And when Don Garci's sermon
Thrilled through his hearers, he
Could hear the vast crowd's murmur,
As of a human tree.

"The gorgeous windows painted
The banner of the dead.
Then to himself this heathen
Began to think, and said:
'This is that valiant body

199

Which, living, all men feared!
Now, Cid, what harm befalls him
Who plucks you by the beard?'
"One step he takes advancing;
He lifts his hand and sneers
Ah me, what shrieks of terror
Are these the Abbot hears?
What screams for help and mercy,
That ring so long and loud?
The Abbot leaves his preachment,
And hastens through the crowd.

"Within the silent chapel,
Before the ivory throne,
Livid with fright and lifeless,
The Jew lay stark as stone.
For to! the tall dead hero
Had shifted his right hand;
A palm's-breadth from the scabbard
Had drawn the mighty brand;
The mantle-strings had loosened,
The mantle dropped to ground,
As, starting on the dastard,
The Cid had risen, and frowned."

Cries of applause greeted the close of the song but Israel the gunner, drawing up his tall figure from the bulwarks on which he had been leaning, turned to Pedro. "The Jews, Pedro Galdos," he began in quiet tones, but before he could go further, the singer sprang towards him with open hand. "Pardon brother," he cried earnestly, "pardon! I had forgotten. So long have you been one of us that no one remembered."

"That is well said, brother," replied Israel. "To me you meant no scorn, nor indeed perchance to any son of Abraham. But songs such as these make black blood between people and people, when God knows there is little need. In the old days, *caballeros*, an evil king came against Israel with the noise of a great multitude, horsemen in thousands, and men in mail, and elephants bearing castles on their backs; and the mountains blazed like fire as the sun flashed on the shields of brass and gold. There was but a little band to withstand them, but Eleazar Avaran saw that one of the great beasts stood higher than the rest, and that its huge body glittered with royal bucklers; and thinking that the king was in the castle which the beast carried, he leaped forward and fought with the mailed men that marched before the beast. On this side and that he slew them until they divided and gave way on either hand. Then he ran under the beast, and thrust mightily upward, and took the life of it. As it sank down dead it fell upon him, and so Eleazar Avaran gave his life for Israel."

"By the horn of the unicorn—and the Lord deliver us from it!" cried Patricio, the wild man with ruddy hair, merry blue eyes, and long upper lip, "'twas a noble death, and the man a hero, God rest his soul!"

"When this king's father was king before him," continued the gunner, "and the heathen revelled in the temple of the Lord, and the children of Israel were constrained to go crowned with ivy and roses and vine leaves in the processions of the false gods and to eat of the meats offered to idols, there was a woman with seven sons who would do none of these things. She and her sons were taken before the king; and the eldest son was scourged and tortured and slain with fire, before the face of his mother and his brethren. One after another they took her sons, and maimed and slew them, while she stood by with her hope set on the Lord, and bade them be of good courage for the sake of the Law. When they came to the last of the sons, the king said, 'Thou art but a lad, and the light is pleasant to the young, and thy mother has no other left her but thee; eat and live.' And when the king could not win him to his will either by wealth or power or promise of friendship, he said to the mother, 'Speak thou to him, he is thy youngest and the last of thy children; bid him save himself.' 'I will speak to him,' said the woman gladly, and laughed scornfully at the king. 'Dear son,' she said, in the speech of her fathers, 'have pity on me who bore you, and for three years suckled you, and nourished and reared you unto these days. Lift up

A Child's Book of Warriors

your eyes, dear child, and see the things in heaven and earth all made by God out of nought, and the children of men with them. Have no fear of this butcher; show yourself worthy of your brothers, so that in God's mercy I may receive you again with them.' Then said the lad, 'Why do we wait?' and he rebuked the king to his face, and was tortured still more cruelly than the others. And when they had slain him, they slew the mother also. The Jew has no country now, *caballeros*, but Israel has still men brave as Eleazar, and women as noble as this mother without a name."

"By the horn of the unicorn and the jewel that's into it," exclaimed Patricio, "the lady was the better man, señor gunner. A most enchanting and magnanimous lady!—like Queen Maev herself, and who should know but me that's a king's son in my own country? I am telling you, boys and *caballeros*, there's not a country on all the big flat of the world that has not its champions and its fine women to it. And why not? Did not the Lord in heaven make us all of the one clay and moisten the clay with the one river of the garden, and blow His own blessed breath into it? And so He did."

"That is a true word, Don Patricio," said Gioia the Sicilian. "In my country where I was born—and that's in Sicily—on the other side of the river there are mounds and broken pillars of marble. In the ancient times, the priest told me, that was a glorious city, and the governor was Duke Himera. Now a mighty African king came over the seas against it with ten thousand ships, for he wanted to have the city and all the island and then go against Rome and drive out the holy pope, for the king was a pagan. He landed and pitched a great camp and drew up his caravels and round ships on the shore, and the fighting began, and Duke Himera had a bad time of it. But on a day they brought in a prisoner, and he told the duke that one of the western cities in the island had turned traitor, and was sending the African a body of horsemen to help him."

"That reminds me now," said Patricio; "go on sir, go on; I won't interrupt you."

"Well, the duke laughed and clapped his hands together at the news. He sent out his own horsemen under cloud of night, and they fetched a round through the hills, and came to the African camp in the twilight of the morning. 'We are the cavalry from the west,' said they, and the Africans threw open the camp-gates to them with shouts of joy. But before any one could guess what they were about, the horsemen galloped down to the shore and set the ships on fire, and then they began to slaughter. When the clouds of smoke and flame were seen from the city, Duke Himera and his troops rushed out against the enemy; and all that day there was mighty fighting along the sea-shore.

"This way and that the battle swung like a wood in the wind; now it was the duke winning, and now it was the invaders. And all that day the African king stood beside a great altar of fire on the high ground of the camp and sacrificed living men to his gods. Hour after hour the strife went on with changing fortunes, but as the bloody day drew to its end the Africans began to give way, and Himera to drive them to the sea and the wrecks of the smoking ships. Then the African king saw at last that his kingdom had been taken from him, and lifting up his hands, he raised a wild chant to the setting sun, and cast himself into the great fire."

"By the horn of the unicorn and his collar of gold," cried Patricio, "he was a glorious old sinner, the heavens be his bed! for sure the Lord knew it was Himself the man would be worshipping, but hadn't heard His name. Now, boys and *caballeros*, these horsemen of the duke brought to memory an old story of one of the kings in my country, and who should remember it better than myself that's a king's son, now in exile? Will ye hear it? Long and long ago then, on a summer evening, a rider on horseback came to a poor cabin on the morning side of the green hills of Wicklow. The man of the cabin was working on his bit of land, and he looked up at the sound of the hoofs. 'A good day to you, and the blessing of God,' says the rider; 'where's the woman of the cabin?' 'She's within doors,' said the man. 'Then tell her she's wanted,' and when the woman came the rider throws back his cloak, and there was a child in the bend of his arm. 'Take it,' says he, 'and don't let it fall. It's two years old he is, and you'll call him Brian the Red. Here's a bag of silver with him, and you'll bring him up kindly for your own child, till I come this way again.' Before the woman could find a word, the rider was galloping off into the hills, and there was the boy in her arms laughing up in her face.

"Now, *caballeros*, when Brian the Red was five years old, this mother of his brought him from the fair a wooden horse that went on wheels, for it was of horses and of horses that the small soul was talking day in and day out. 'Sure then,' says she, 'it's a king's son he is, and a horse he shall have, if I have to go bare for it.' After that, up and down goes Brian the Red, dragging his horse after him, and talking to him, and putting words into the creature's mouth to answer himself.

"A mile or more from the cabin there was a fairy fort, and who steps boldly into it but Brian, and sits down on the grass, and gives his horse handfuls of the grass to eat? But somehow that day it comes upon him that the horse is only bits of wood pinned together, and not a living creature at all. With that he flings him on one side, and lets out a mighty cry of misery. In a moment a green turf of the mound is tilted up, and out looks a woman's face, small as small but pretty as you please. 'Are you hungry, now, bright pulse of my heart? ' says she. 'I am not, thank you kindly,' says Brian. 'Then why are you bawling, my darling?' says she. 'The horse is wood, and can't go,' says the soul, 'and he's not a horse at all,' and began to roar again. 'Was it a real live horse you wanted?' 'Sure, then, I'm a real live boy,' he answers. 'Get on your feet then, hero-boy,' says she laughing, 'for here is one that will teach you the horseman's word and the foal's cry, and make you a lord of horses.'

"Out of the green window of the fairy fort looks a little merry man of the 'good people' and calls the lad to him. 'Listen now,' says he, 'and remember. This is the horseman's word, and the horse that hears it will break bounds or kill himself but he will come to you. And he will follow you like a lamb and love you truer than a woman. But keep the word for his own ear.' And when the little man had whispered the word, 'This,' says he, 'is the foal's cry, and never a mare in the world but will come to you at the sound of it, uproarious and fighting-mad to protect its young—and that's you, my son, until you appease it with the horseman's word. Away now, and get what you want. Yonder in the hollow of the Grassy Land are the King of Wicklow's horses.' 'Are they big? ' asks the soul. 'The King of Wicklow's stallion is the biggest beast in the world.' 'Thank you, lady; and thank you, sir,' says Brian, and picks up his wooden horse, and trots away with joy in the eyes of him.

"In the grey of the next day in the morning comes up the soul out of the hollow of the Grassy Land, with the mighty stallion walking like a mountain by the side of him, and stops at the cabin. 'Come out, mother, and look at him,' he shouts; 'he's a real horse and the biggest in the world.' 'Where did you get him from?' asks the man of the cabin. 'Sure, he's the King of Wicklow's stallion,' says Brian, 'and I got him on the Grassy Land.' 'Ochone, ochone! ' cries the woman; 'it's a killed boy you will be, stealing the king's stallion.' 'I didn't steal him,' says Brian; 'he just came with me.'

"Away to court goes the poor man, all trembling. The countryside was astir, seeking high and low for the King of Wicklow's mighty horse; and to make a long story short, the man tells the king's warriors where they will find the stallion. 'You can't take him without me,' says Brian when they got to the cabin. And sure they could not, for the stallion lays back his ears, and bares his white teeth, and lashes out when any one steps near. 'Put me on his back,' says the soul, 'and it's quiet as a lamb he'll go;' and 'Whoa!' says he to the stallion. A tall soldier lifts the lad on to the beast's back, and the stallion whinnies with pleasure at the feel of him.

"'Why did you steal the best of my horses?' said the King of Wicklow. 'Sure, King of Wicklow dear, steal him I did not, but I spoke to him and he came with me. And if you think I couldn't have taken the others, I could.' 'Could you then?' says the king, wondering at the queerness and the boldness of the soul. 'Then and now,' says Brian, 'but I didn't want them.' 'What for did you want this one? ' says the king. 'Look,' says Brian, holding out his wooden horse, 'this is the only horse I had, and it can't go, and it is not alive, and it's not as big as myself.' 'It is not,' says the king; 'what do you keep it for?' 'Ah, well,' says Brian, hugging it to him, 'it's a fine horse when you make believe, and he's an old friend.' 'Whose lad is this?' asked the king. 'That's a secret mystery, King of

Wicklow,' says the woman of the cabin, and tells him how the soul was brought to them. 'When was that?' asked the king eagerly. 'Three years ago and more it was,' says the woman. 'Glory be to the Father,' cries the king, 'it's my own boy that was stolen.' With that he hugs the lad to him, and there was great rejoicing from the green hills of Wicklow to the sea.

"Ever after the lad was free to go among the horses and play with them as he liked. When some time had gone by, there was war broke out with the King of Meath, and that king sent down a great host with chariots and horses against the King of Wicklow. 'Father,' says Brian, 'I will give you this battle for nothing if you like.' 'How will you do that?' asks the king. 'Sure then,' says the hero-boy, 'I will stand on the hillside, and as the King of Meath goes by with his horses and chariots, I will let out the cry of the foal, and there is not a mare but will turn and run to me, and in the confusion you can fall on the King of Meath.' By the horn—"

But before Patricio could cry out, "A light!" the voice of Rodriguez of Triana came ringing from the bows, "Land ho! Land!"

Far away to the west gleamed a light which rose and fell, as though it were a torch burning on a fishing-boat at sea. Beyond the light rose a dim outline of land, making a blank among the low stars, yet itself scarcely visible in the blue-green sky.

"Fire a gun," said the captain, "and let the admiral know we have won;" and Israel the gunner lit the first powder burnt in those western seas.

The caravels shortened sail and lay-to until day. In the blaze of the morning sun, when the air blew sweet as the breath of spring in Andalusia, and only the nightingales were wanting, the boats' dashed in to a long green isle covered with new-world trees.

A tall man, ruddy and fair, with blue eyes and long hair white as silver, was the first to leap ashore, to fall on his knees and kiss the earth. It was the Admiral Cristobal Colon. Drawing his sword and spreading the royal standard of the green cross, he took possession of the island in the name of the sovereigns of Castile. As he returned thanks to God for all

His mercies, one thought ran uppermost in his mind: Now surely, O Lord, I shall live to free the land of Thy holy sepulchre. That was really the dream of his life; and his search for the Land of Gold and Spices was undertaken to provide him with the means of attaining his end.

Our last story was told on Twelfth Night, and the snow was deep on the ground.

"And this is the last of the apple-tree fires," said the Truthful Story-teller, who had measured his magic fuel to suit the stories.

"Is there no more of that lovely old apple-wood?" exclaimed Beatrice. "Oh, what a pity!"

"I like it," said Vigdis emphatically, "it *is* warm! Doesn't it bring back the breezy summer days when the crows went sailing over, and we heard the apples dropping?"

"What ages ago it all seems!" said Beatrice. "Do you mind how Hedgehog escaped into the plantation, and we went hunting for him?"

"I wonder where Hog o' the Hedge is now. Wasn't he a spiky old bird?"—this from Simplicia.

"And Giggums came after us," continued Beatrice, "and we both nearly died of laughing, doing Claribel!"

"My dears!" exclaimed mother. "Spiky bird! Doing Claribel!"

"Oh, you sweet thing!" cried Simplicia, "that's Tennyson—

"'Where Claribel low-lieth;'

like Brer Rabbit, only Claribel sounds nicer!"

At which mother heaved a tragic sigh, and the Truthful Story-teller laughed, and we all went on chattering nonsense till it was quite late.

"*Must* you go to-morrow, Beatrice?" asked Vigdis; "I *am* sorry."

"So am I," said Simplicia; "we must try to live without you."

"Oh, I shall be back in July," rejoined Beatrice cheerily.

"Then we must try to live with you," said Simplicia.

Whereupon these two rushed gleefully at each other, and closed in the hug practised by the Giant Wrestlers.

Whereupon also, the Truthful Story-teller, referring ironically to bear-gardens and other select places of amusement, wrapped up, and went out into the snow with Sigfrid. For, as it has been noted, it was Twelfth Night; and when the roads are white and the flakes falling, the words "Twelfth Night" are like a magic pipe leading back to old snowy winters, and Elizabethan revels, and the hills from which the turbaned kings and the horses and camels come winding in Orient splendour in Fabriano's altar-piece of the Magi at Bethlehem.